Discovering the Yorkshire Dales

Already published:
Discovering Aberdeenshire
Discovering Angus & The Mearns
Discovering Argyll, Mull & Iona
Discovering The Black Isle
Discovering The Cotswolds
Discovering Cumbria
Discovering Dumfriesshire
Discovering East Lothian
Discovering Fife
Discovering Galloway
Discovering Inverness-shire
Discovering Lancashire – 1. The Coast
Discovering Lancashire – 2. Inland
Discovering Lewis and Harris
Discovering The Pentland Hills
Discovering Speyside
Discovering The Water of Leith
Discovering West Lothian

Discovering the Yorkshire Dales

RON & MARLENE FREETHY

JOHN DONALD PUBLISHERS LTD
EDINBURGH

ISBN 0 85976 327 7

British Library Cataloguing in Publication Data
Freethy, Ron
    Discovering the Yorkshire Dales.
    1. Yorkshire (England)
    I. Title II. Freethy, Marlene
    914.28104859

Phototypeset by Newtext Composition Ltd, Glasgow.
Printed & bound in Great Britain by Bell & Bain Ltd, Glasgow.

Acknowledgements

This is not a book about the Yorkshire Dales National Park, it is a book about The Yorkshire Dales, its moorlands, its rivers, its history, its fauna and flora and its people. The area described could perhaps best be called Yorkshire's river valleys, for nowhere in Britain is there a better collection of delightfully varied watercourses.

Some may ask what pursuaded a Lancastrian and a Cumbrian to write a book about Yorkshire. The answer is that whilst we may poke fun at each other, these counties are full of northern grit and we will defend each other against the rest of the world.

For the last twenty years we have lived within a few miles of the Yorkshire Dales and have found sanctuary and quiet roads in the Dales when the traffic on the motorways to the south is bumper to bumper for miles. We have been lucky in our choice of friends who have shared with us their knowledge and enthusiasm. Brian Lee is a half-breed with a Lancastrian father and a mother from the other side. In his knowledgeable company we have driven up and down each dale and walked for miles looking at the ruins of lead mines and abbeys, castles and churches, woodlands and winding paths. To Miriam Wright of Grassington who is related to the Keartons and to the lead-mining historian Edward Fawcett we extend our thanks. Renée Donley has given us great assistance and helped us to explore the county of her birth more than she realises, and for this we are grateful. To the many tourist information officers, librarians and curators of museums we say a heartfelt 'thank you' for answering our many questions and searching out references without grumbling out loud.

We are pleased that our son Paul has decided to live and work in Yorkshire, thus developing his own love for the Dales, and we are grateful to him for his photographic help.

Our only regret is that lack of space has prevented the inclusion of all the delights of the Dales, but we hope that what has been included will persuade our readers to polish their walking boots and head for the beauty and friendliness of Yorkshire.

R. & M.F.

Contents

	Page
Acknowledgements	v
1. Geology, Industry and Natural History	1
2. The Craven Dales	19
3. Upper Ribblesdale	31
4. Malham and Airedale	47
5. Wharfedale	67
6. The Ure and Wensleydale	89
7. Around Ripon	111
8. Nidderdale	121
9. Swaledale	145
Further Reading	164
Index	165

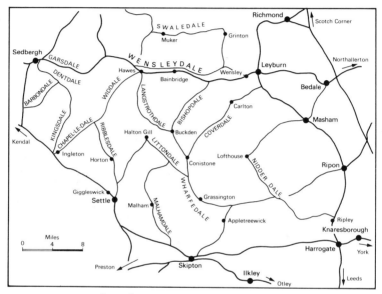

Location Map: The Yorkshire Dales.

CHAPTER 1

Geology, Industry and Natural History

Lovers of limestone scenery have always found the Yorkshire Dales irresistible. The area drains quickly and this usually ensures dry walking, but the fact that rainwater is a dilute solution of carbonic acid has caused the limestone to dissolve over millions of years, thus producing some of the finest underground cave systems in Britain. Some show caves are now safely open to the public, particularly at Ingleton, Clapham and at Stump Cross between Wharfedale and Nidderdale. Geologists refer to the huge slab of limestone making up the Yorkshire Dales as the Askrigg Block.

Limestone was formed mainly during the Carboniferous Period which began about 350 million years ago when conditions were warm and the tropical seas abounded with life, many of the animals having shells composed mainly of calcium carbonate. Typical of these were the crinoids or sea lilies which were actually animals anchored to the sea bed and which fed by waving their 'arms' about and catching microscopic plants. Once captured, the food was propelled down to the mouth by the beating of small hair-like structures called cilia. The sheer bulk of these sea lilies and other similar species plus the relatives of modern-day squids and snails produced huge deposits of shells from the dead animals. These sank to the bottom of the sea and covered up the older rocks on the bed. After about 50 million years these layered limestone deposits were thrust upwards by earthquakes and volcanic eruptions, and the seas became ever shallower and eventually evaporated, leaving the limestone areas typical of the Dales. Areas where millstone grit is found, such as in parts of the Dales, the Pennines and Southern Scotland, indicates the presence of once-extensive estuaries into which huge rivers dumped sediments eroded from the upland rocks.

The Askrigg Block is exposed in many places, and a close look at the faces of rock will reveal thousands of marine fossils. The centre of the block is actually beneath Askrigg in

1

Wensleydale, hence its name. To the south of the main block is the so-called Craven Fault of which there are three branches. By far the longest is the North Craven Fault which stretches from the west at Ingleton to the east at Pateley Bridge in Nidderdale. Running parallel to this is the Mid-Craven Fault, and this is joined at Settle by the South Craven Fault which runs south-west to Skipton. The road out of Settle towards Ingleton up Buckhaw Brow follows the line of the South Craven Fault and there is an obvious change in vegetation from one side of the road to the other. There is limestone to the right of the climb and millstone grit to the left. Until early in 1990 it was a risk to do this, but the new bypass has meant that the old road is now much quieter and safer. All the land to the north of these faults has been thrust upwards, and the movements have not quite stopped, as we and many others discovered in the early 1970s as we were thrown out of bed in the early hours of the morning as the Craven Fault moved. The odd disturbance is perhaps acceptable as the faults have over millions of years produced the wonderful scenery of Giggleswick, Goredale and the dramatic Malham Cove.

It was the Ice Age or rather the period during which it melted which did most to structure the Dales. After a long and complex ebb and flow the retreat of the ice began in earnest about 10,000 years ago and the slow-moving glaciers carried not only light detritus but also larger boulders called erratics which were left stranded. The mountains, of which the area has several, were the source of glaciers especially around Wild Boar, Baugh and Great Shunner Fells. The ice ground its remorseless way radially outwards, its passage recorded by deep scratch marks on the rocks. Another way of working out the route of the ice is to examine the alignment of drumlins, which are hillocks of boulder clay left behind as the ice melted. This is a particular feature of Upper Ribblesdale on the Horton to Ribblehead road to the north of Selside. Here the drumlins lie in a north-easterly/south-westerly direction. Further down the valley the drumlins lie north–south, thus proving that the ice split in two around Ribblehead, one branch gouging out Ribblesdale and the other forming the Greta Valley towards Ingleton.

Glacial drift has affected the scenery because it restricts the

A typical area of limestone pavement above Grassington.

natural drainage and can in extreme cases deflect a river. This has happened in Wensleydale where two tributary streams of the Ure – Fossdale Gill and Hearne Beck – have been diverted to the east. They have then combined and plunge over Hardraw Scar. Cotter Force has been produced in the same way with Cotterdale Beck being impeded by glacial deposits.

In summary we can say that the Dales' scenery is composed mainly of limestone formed in warm shallow seas and later gouged into U-shaped valleys by the ice. The main valleys are those of the Ribble, Aire (Airedale and Malhamdale), Wharfe, Nidd, the Ure (Wensleydale) and Swale.

In the 10,000 years since the final retreat of the ice there have obviously been climatic changes, but nothing dramatic enough to disturb the steady ecological succession. Following the ice, tundra conditions prevailed with the dominant vegetation being dwarf willow, dwarf birch and lichens. Fossils and cave deposits, especially from the Victoria cave above Settle, prove the presence of woolly rhinoceros and mammoths which literally scraped an existence from the vegetation.

About 8,000 years ago the climate became warmer and drier and trees could gain a root hold even on the high moors where birch was dominant, but there was also some oak and ash.

3

Lily-of-the valley.

Scientists have been able to back up their theories by hard evidence because each plant species has its own uniquely shaped pollen grains. These tiny structures are very tough, survive in oxygen-deficient peat bogs and can be radiocarbondated. With each plant having its own 'fingerprint' it is possible to identify pollen grain shape and also to carry out counts from which the relative dominance of the various species can be worked out. In the valley areas woodlands of pine, hazel, oak, elm, and lime flourished with alder dominating the wetter areas. Wild oxen grazed on the moors whilst the woodlands supported bear, wild boar, wolves, probably lynx, and wild cat plus several species of deer. Otters were common in the rivers which also supported beavers until Saxon times – indeed Beverley in Yorkshire takes its name from this animal. The list of small mammals would not be significantly different from those found today except that there would be no mice or rats,

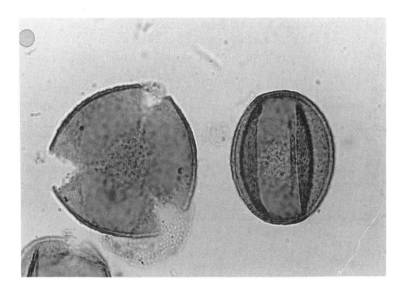

Pollen grains of oak (above) and pine (below).

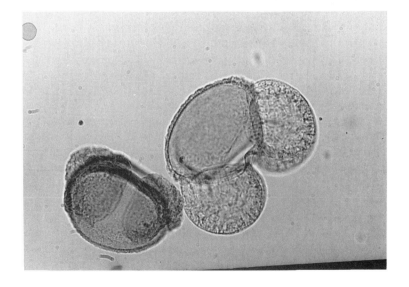

which were Asiatic or southern European species which came to England along the medieval trade routes.

Around 7,500 years ago conditions became wetter, and by 5,000 years ago the temperature had fallen with the result that oak declined and birch and alder became much more common. By this time, however, human activities began to have some effect on the landscape and the pollen from cultivated grasses and cereals proves this. This means that forest clearing to produce fields had begun.

The first human settlers in the Dales probably did little damage to the landscape, and exploitation of its rich resources probably began with the Romans. Pigs of lead, dating from AD81, have been found stamped BRIG, indicating BRIGANTIA, a region of pre-Roman Britain, the name of which the invaders retained. Lead occurs mostly in the form of its sulphide known as galena which has the external appearance of the metal itself except that it is much more brittle. Zinc is found in similar areas, occurring as a brownish resin-like zinc blend also called sphalerite. But it was lead which was important, and the other ores were referred to as gangue and were dumped, thus creating huge spoil heaps. Barite was one of the gangue ores and is white and very heavy. Also dumped, but in smaller quantities, was flourspar, a transparent cubic material very variable in colour, but in Derbyshire it is bluish-purple and is called Blue-John. Calcite, occurring in rhombic-shaped crystals, is a very pure form of calcium carbonate, with the same formula as limestone, although the calcite is invariably stained brown.

Few of these minerals were ever exploited commercially and the search for lead was the driving force of the early industrial developers of the Dales. Finding the metal was one thing, but getting at it was another. The development of mining techniques and efficient drainage in particular were slow in coming, and it was only the development of steam engines which enabled the miners to penetrate the deeper seams. Once production problems were overcome, serious pollution problems at the surface became inevitable. Huge spoil heaps began to dominate the landscape and prevented grazing by sheep and cattle, which were affected by the lead. Many plants would not grow in these areas either. What is amazing is that

Stump Cross Cavern – one of the best limestone show caves in the Dales.

some plants, including the delicate white blossoms of spring sandwort, grow well on the spoil heaps, and some geologists have used its presence to prospect successfully for lead in previously untapped areas. In the early days the smelting methods were primitive, to say the least, and clouds of poisonous fumes containing cadmium, sulphuorous gases and cyanide (now recognised respectively as cancer causer, acid rain producer and deadly poison) billowed across the landscape. Very large areas soon became totally unfit for farming, especially round Grassington. Farmers complained so bitterly that a long underground complex of flues and condensers were constructed not only to spread the fumes but also to collect saleable by-products such as arsenic. We can only pity the poor souls whose job it was to collect the arsenic.

If glaciation had its effect upon the landscape of the Dales, then the same can be said of the 'Old Men' as the miners were called. There is still plenty of evidence of their surface 'hushes' which involved damming a stream until a head of water built up behind it. They then released the water, producing sufficient power to wear away the top soil and loose rock to reveal the mineral-bearing ores beneath. These are a particular feature of Swaledale where they are often confused with dry

The common lizard finds the stone walls and dints of limestone of the dales ideal places to bask in the sunshine.

valleys or glacial overflows. Our favourite such area is called the Hungry Hushes, which may well indicate that the exposed rocks were not as rich as the Old Men had anticipated. Once the veins had been exposed, they still had to be excavated, and the most frequently used early method involved digging bell pits. These were, as the name implies, bell-shaped scrapes from which the ore had been extracted. In limestone country they can be confused with 'swallow holes' which are caused when water below limestone dissolves the rock and the thin layer of surface soil falls into the depression. A miner's bell pit, however, can be easily recognised because it is surrounded by a circular ring of gangue plus the associated lead-loving plants. When a system of bell pits proved to be profitable, a channel was dug between them along the vein with gangue thrown out on either side just as modern workers do when laying a pipeline. Such diggings were known as coffin work.

Once all surface sources had been tapped, the miners had to take ever greater risks and sink ever deeper shafts. To locate these shafts it is best to stand upon elevated ground and look round with binoculars for an area from which spoil heaps seem to radiate. The actual shafts are obviously dangerous and should never be entered, and even one inquisitive stride into the entrance should be resisted. Initially wooden ladders fastened together descended into the workings and buckets of ore were carried up or wound up by rope. Steam power changed all this and sophisticated winding gear was used to lift the crude ores from deep shafts which were always flooding, with ventilation always a problem. Naked lights, however, could be used since there was no problem with methane gas which has always been the coal miners' greatest threat. The necessary skills needed to mine at depth were not present in Britain, and many German miners were engaged to bring their experience to bear. They constructed gently sloping tunnels called levels, beginning from the lowest point available in a valley, and then other lower drainage and ventilation levels were cut. These also provided a convenient route for the removal of crude ore from the workings. The entrances to these levels are easy to find as they were usually arched and constructed of stone or brick. Botanists find these shady spots ideal for mosses and ferns, especially harts tongue, common polypody, wall rue and maidenhair spleenwort.

Once a rich vein of lead had been discovered and mined, the industrialists' problem was far from over since the ore had to be smelted, and this required fuel. There was no problem in the early days as the mine owner simply negotiated timber rights with the local landowner, although in many cases this was not necessary as the two were one and the same. Inevitably, though, the desire for profit blinded common sense and the landscape became almost denuded of trees and clouded in acrid fumes. It is hard for us to think that one of Britain's most beautiful tourist areas was once a blackspot of industrial pollution. The moorland smelters had soon to turn to alternative fuel supplies and initially they reverted to the use of peat, but the Grassington works could obtain supplies of coal from nearby Threshfield, Swaledale and there were also good supplies on Tan Hill. The latter source had been tapped by the monks of Jervaulx, Coverham and Bolton as well as the owners of Richmond Castle, and no doubt lesser establishments were

Birds eye primrose.

not slow to follow suit. At Tan Hill the German method of drift mining was adopted where there were outcrops, especially above the Kettlepot Ganister and Upper Howgate Edge. These were not of very high quality but served a vital purpose until the coming of the railway allowed better coal to be brought in from Durham and Northumberland. One Tan Hill coal mine, however, remained in business until the 1940s and thus outlasted all of the lead mines which had ceased to function more than thirty years before.

If mining is a thing of the past, then quarrying, probably an even older industry, is very much part of the Dalesman's future and is likely to bring him more and more into conflict with the conservationists. Quarries provided stone for walls and buildings, for road construction and for lime burning. Good-quality limestone was required for buildings with other substantial slabs being ideal for the construction of stone walls which are so much a feature of the now treeless Dales landscape. Visitors should keep an eye open at the various Tourist Information Centres, as the Yorkshire Dales National Park Authority often organise stone-walling days during which an expert demonstrates the basic techniques to total novices.

Once the builder and waller had selected their material, the rest of the rough stone was used for road building and repair. These days large, but we stress necessary, quarries scar the landscape but old disused workings, long since grassed over, are present around most villages and are now a haven for wildlife. It is surprising how quickly nature can heal the wounds caused by human activities. The areas of controversy are the large quarries especially around Horton-in-Ribblesdale which tourists, weekend cottage owners and affluent residents commuting to town jobs complain are noisy, dirty and unsightly, not to mention the ear-shattering noise of the occasional blasting. In reply we must ask, how else do we obtain building material for roads and airports, so essential to our commerce, and where else do locals find employment? It is mostly the workers' pay which supports local pubs and shops, their children who keep the village schools open, and their families who support the church. We feel that the Dales villages should live as they have always done – on and off the land. But some compromises should be made in the face of a thankfully more conservation-minded world. Nature should be given a hand to repair the damage, and ecologically sensitive areas should be identified prior to commencement or extension of mining, thus ensuring that industry and wildlife are able to exist side by side.

Farming is an industry which no longer depends upon quarrying; at one time every Dales village had at least one lime

Emperor moth.

kiln. The lime was used to improve the land by discouraging the growth of heather, rushes and bracken which grow best on acid soils. A growth of lusher grass was therefore encouraged, but the amount of lime used had to be carefully regulated, and there was an old saying that "too much lime makes a farmer rich and his son poor". These days the insensitive use of modern chemicals may be producing similar problems. The kilns resemble a stubby tower with a substantial hearth at the base. Limestone was mixed with local peat or wood with coal eventually being bought for the purpose, and this was pushed into the top of the kiln. The fire was lit from below and was kept going by adding more materials from above and raking out the lime from below. Once the cinders had been riddled out, the lime was slaked before being spread on the land.

The human impact on the land has been far-reaching, and this continues today with the increasing numbers of tourists who explore the narrow roads, and look for toilets, cafes, historic ruins, caves, caravan sites, picnic areas, hotels and quiet spots. The last two are rather elusive. There have never been many large hotels in the Dales, and too many would certainly spoil the area and reduce the number of quiet spots from a few to none at all and put the wildlife under even greater pressure.

Without doubt the real joy of the Dales to the naturalist are the flowers, especially those of the upland areas of limestone pavement. Three of the best examples of this are above Malham, on Grassington Moor and around Austwick. They consist of blocks of limestone called clints with the gaps between being known as grykes, and these have been responsible for many a broken ankle when unwary visitors try to move too quickly. The grykes tend to develop their own little ecosystem, retaining water and holding soil in the shelter away from the wind. Here grow many ferns, some of them, like the limestone polypody, quite rare, and flowering plants such as the common shining cranesbill and the rare baneberry. This poisonous plant, at one time known as Herb Christopher, was used to produce a black dye. During Victorian times there was a craze for collecting ferns and keeping them in glass containers almost like a transparent gryke, which this led to speculators selling the plants, thus reducing the rare species almost to extinction. In the 1990s gardening is popular and no self-respecting horticulturalist can afford to be without a limestone rockery. Until laws were passed to prevent it, large areas of limestone pavement were lifted and transported to be sold from garden centres. On warm days limestone pavements are ideal places to picnic and cold-blooded creatures such as lizards also use the clints as basking areas early in the morning in order to raise their temperature and enable them to move quickly enough to catch their prey.

In some areas the limestone is covered by a thin layer of soil and these grassland meadows also support a great variety of flowers including the surprisingly large and colourful mountain pansy, the slim pink stands of birds eye primrose and in a few places the insignificant and difficult-to-find creamy flowers of the Yorkshire milkwort. Other species include limestone bedstraw, fairy flax, hairy rock cress, rock rose and three saxifrages – meadow, mossy and rue-leaved. We once set off with a botanist friend to walk the limestone meadows above Grassington. We covered two miles in eight hours, ran out of film, but finished up with a fine collection of limestone-loving flowers.

Some limestone areas in the Dales are capped with heather, which is disconcerting as botanists are taught that heather is acid-loving. The reason for its presence is drainage, the water percolating through the limestone, leaching the bases from the soil and leaving it acid. A layer of peaty soil can thus develop, and in addition to the heathers, cotton grass, bilberry, bearberry, tormentil, heath bedstraw, marsh pennywort, bog pimpernel, lesser twayblade and an assortment of rushes also grow. The attractive emperor moth has larvae which feed upon the heather.

Where outcrops of rock, locally known as scars, are exposed and weathered, the rocks on which the limestone is resting are exposed. These harder, older siliceous rocks do not erode so quickly and alkaline water emerging from the scar produces 'flushes' which are always exciting places for botanists.

The Dales still have a number of interesting limestone-based woodlands amongst which are found Britain's rarest plant, the Lady's Slipper Orchid, its two sites being sensibly guarded secrets protected by wardens in tents and a complex of trip wires. Interesting woodlands include Colt Park in Upper Ribblesdale, administered by the Nature Conservancy Council, Bolton Woods which is open on payment of a small fee, and Grass Wood near Grassington which is freely open at all times. The list of flowers here is impressive and includes lily of the valley, woodruff, saw-wort, melancholy thistle, wood geranium, herb paris, and nodding melic grass.

Whilst the plants are the most significant part of the natural history, the animal life is also exciting at times, with the limestone attracting a variety of snails which make use of it for their shells and the hardness of the river water ensuring a rich variety of aquatic invertebrates such as stonefly, mayfly, caddis fly and the crayfish. The water shrew feeds upon such creatures and therefore also requires an unpolluted habitat. The contrast between its dark upper surface and paler belly is obvious, as are the hairy keel on the underside of the tail and the paddle-like hairs which fringe the hind feet. We were once watching a water shrew on a hot August day when we were surprised to see a hedgehog swimming across the River Ure close to Hawes.

Brown hares are common in the Dales, and so were rabbits until they were reduced by the 1953 outbreak of myxomatosis. There was a dramatic improvement in the 1980s and we counted over 500 basking outside their burrows in the evening September sun during an enchantingly slow drive up Littondale. Foxes are common everywhere and badgers have setts which have been inhabited for centuries, often penetrating deep into the limestone rocks. There has been a sad decline in the otter population and a worrying increase in the number of mink which have escaped from the once-common fur farms, and they have now firmly established themselves.

Ornithologists have to work hard for their birds in the Dales, especially for predators which have been persecuted for many years on the moors which are devoted to the rearing of grouse in preparation for the glorious 12th of August! The graceful peregrine, the swift and low-flying merlin, the short-eared owl and the hen harrier were all pole-trapped, poisoned and shot by gamekeepers whose jobs depended upon a successful grouse shoot on their masters' estates with guests frequently including Royalty. Nowadays many of the marksmen are German businessmen, but in any case there is a much more realistic attitude to predatory birds, as published scientific work shows how little they actually affect the young grouse.

Upland breeding species include curlew, golden plover, lapwing, meadow pipit, skylark, and the wheatear which arrives in April, its prominent white rump being easily seen as it bobs up and down on a stone. Down on the swift-flowing rivers the white-bibbed bobbing dipper is more common than the more colourful kingfisher, which requires pools with overhanging vegetation to provide a diving platform.

Curlew.

The resident grey wagtail frequents the shallows and the summer-visiting yellow wagtail, looking canary-like in its plumage, breeds in the water meadows. Woodland species include the jay, great spotted woodpecker and treecreeper, plus the nuthatch and pied flycatcher, both increasingly common in Bolton Woods along the Wharfe.

In this area we also watched a Daubenton's bat hawking for insects along the river on a warm August evening. On another memorable evening in May we stood spellbound as thousands of mayflies emerged from their underwater pupae to enjoy one brief period of mating in flight before the female lays her eggs which develop in the water. Small wonder scientists have named the mayfly family the Ephemenoptera. The trout were not slow to notice the rise of the mayfly and they lashed the water into a creamy foam in their eagerness to feed. On yet another day of high wind and rain we saw nothing and yet enjoyed taking shelter and studying the architecture of the Priory set close to the river. This is the joy of the Dales – there is something for everybody at all times. And above all the area offers a working environment for many people, and therefore it feels lived in.

The bee orchid is found in many of the Dales, especially in sheltered limestone areas.

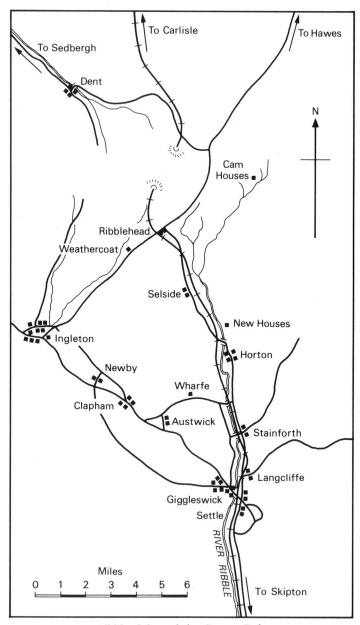

To Carlisle

To Hawes

To Sedbergh

Dent

N

Cam
Houses

Ribblehead

Weathercoat

Selside

New Houses

Ingleton

Horton

Newby

Wharfe

Clapham

Austwick

Stainforth

Langcliffe

Giggleswick

Settle

RIVER RIBBLE

Miles

0 1 2 3 4 5 6

To Skipton

Ribblesdale and the Craven Dales.

18

CHAPTER 2

The Craven Dales

The Craven Dales, an underrated area is served by three substantial market towns: Skipton in Airedale, Settle in Ribblesdale and Kirkby Lonsdale on the borders of Cumbria and Lancashire. We define the Craven Dales as the area to the east of the A65 road which runs from Skipton to Kirkby Lonsdale. This was constructed in the late eighteenth century as a turnpike passing through Skipton, Gargrave, Hellifield, Long Preston and on to Settle. Its purpose was to link the textile towns of Keighley and Kendal. From Settle it wound through Austwick, Clapham and Ingleton, but gradually during the 1980s and early 1990s a new trunk road has bypassed these once-busy settlements and they have now become quiet backwaters far too often missed by tourists who ask "Where are the Dales?" We must answer – these *are* part of the Dales and a part which should not be missed. The area is dominated by the famous three peaks of Whernside, Ingleborough and Penyghent, the last best described in the chapter on upper Ribblesdale.

When is a hill not a hill? The answer is when it becomes a mountain, and to qualify as such the eminence must exceed 2000 feet (609 metres). The plateau of Ingleton reaches 2373 feet (723 metres) and is the largest outcrop of limestone in Britain. The top is so flat that some have suggested that the 15-acre summit could be used as a sportsfield. There are several routes to the summit, none being particularly strenuous. One path begins at the Hill Inn at Chapel-le-Dale whilst other walkers begin their ascent from Ingleton. We have frequently followed both these routes but our favourite way is via the delightful little village of Clapham. At the foot of and sheltered by Ingleborough's southern slopes a string of settlements grew up including Newby, Newby Cote, Clapham itself, Austwick, Lawkland and Feizor. Of these Clapham must have been the most important as it was here that the parish church now dedicated to St James was established. There is no mention of

Thornton Force, near Ingleton.

Clapham in the Domesday survey but this may well have been an omission because the coverage was by no means comprehensive in the northern areas. In his *History of*

The church at Chapel-le-Dale.

Richmondshire Thomas Whitaker mentions that a church was erected in the parish during the reign of Henry I (1100-1135) and points to the presence of legal documents of 1160, 1165, 1189 and 1190 referring to what appears to have been a long-established church. Obviously there have been many alterations since this time and its most dominant feature is a stout tower built after the devastating Scots raids of around 1220. This served the dual function of protection and religious focus. At this time it was dedicated to St. Michael but for some unknown reason its allegiance was transferred to St John the Apostle.

Close by is a substantial National Park Information Centre and car park. A look at the maps on display shows clearly that the village is sited at the mouth of a small valley called Clapdale. At one time the area was the bed of a glacial lake, and is now divided in two by Fell Beck which rises high on the slopes of Ingleborough. Close to its source the beck plunges 340 feet (104 metres) into the depths of Gaping Gill pothole, emerging from the mouth of a cave which marks the beginning of Clapdale. In its lower reaches the watercourse is called Clapham Beck, and from the Information Centre a well-signposted walk leads across an attractive single-arched footbridge known to the locals as 'T' brokken bridge' and then over a second more substantial span from which there are

Clapham Church.

splendid views of the church. Beyond the church, the sound of crashing water indicates the presence of a substantial series of waterfalls which look so natural that it is hard to realise they are in fact man-made.

The influence of the Farrer family in Clapdale began in the eighteenth century, continuing well into the present century, and was indeed profound and has proved to be permanent. The first to settle in Clapham was Richard Farrer who was born at Chipping in Lancashire in 1687 and came to the village in 1716. He was variously described as a 'yeoman' and a 'gentleman'. Although he made every effort to build up his fortune, he lent too much and was repaid too little and when he died in 1766 he was penniless. But he had sent his sons to Giggleswick school and the sound educational background they received was put to good use. It was Oliver (1742-1808) who put the family on the local map. He first went to London and became a solicitor and a moneylender whose clients included

Packhorse Bridge, Clapham.

the Duke of York. By the time he was forty Oliver was worth £40,000 and had earned the name of Penny Bun Farrer because in his early days he had saved so hard that his meals consisted of a penny bun and pump water! He then used his influence to obtain a lucrative post in Bengal for his brother Thomas, another hard worker who in the next four years amassed a fortune of £60,000. Neither brother had any children and so they began to channel funds to their nephews James, William and Oliver, the issue of the third brother. This had the effect of centralising the family funds and led to the purchase of Ingleborough Hall. As Oliver also died childless, the concentration of funds was focused even more tightly. Between 1805 and 1806 the Farrers planted 10,000 trees around Clapham Beck and they also bought up land as and when it became available. In 1820 they constructed a large dam on Clapham Beck to create a lake and the waterfalls. No doubt the extensive plantings made by the family made an impression on its most famous son, Reginald Farrer (1880-1920), who in a short life became one of Britain's most celebrated botanists. His book on Alpine flowers is remembered and his methods of displaying these species are followed to the present day. In 1970, on the 50th anniversary of his death, the Reginald Farrer Trail was established in his memory and can be followed from the Information Centre. It leads alongside the lake and into the woodlands, after payment of a nominal entry fee collected at a

Wood anemonies grow well in the Dales.

cottage in the yard of a sawmill. The lake is around 40 feet (12 metres) deep with limestone crags to the east which were planted up by Reginald. There are trout in the lake but the bird life is usually not very impressive, probably due to the shade created by the fringing woodland. Within the shady area itself, however, the tawny owl breeds, as do coal tit, treecreeper and goldcrest. The trees planted by the Farrers include Norway spruce, beech and sycamore which seem to thrive on the limestone. The woods are still well managed and a felling and replanting programme ensures that naturalists will continue to enjoy this walk well into the next century. Woodcocks also nest in the open areas created in the shade thrown by the evergreen yew and holly. Geologists are fascinated by the area around the head of the lake where the North Craven Fault crosses Clapdale. Just beyond, instead of limestone, there is a belt of acidic Ordovician rock which

A view of Ingleborough from the walk from Ingleton.

Reginald knew well and where he planted Himalayan bamboo and rhododendron which look delightful in May and June.

Soon after you leave the woodlands the scenery assumes a more open aspect with craggy limestone outcrops becoming more evident as you climb. Growing from cracks in the rock are rowan, ash and especially twisted old hawthorns bent by decades of wind and weather. Ingleborough Cave is also open to the public and was first explored by the Farrer family in 1837. Some of the rock formations have been given fantastic names including Beehive, Pillar Hall and the Sword of Damocles. From the cave the path up to Ingleborough strikes through a scree of moss-covered limestone boulders to Trow Gill which was once itself an impressive cave until its roof fell in many centuries ago. Up towards Rayside is a straddle of woodland growing at around 1300 feet (400 metres) and just about on the present growth limit for larch, ash and sycamore, whilst on the windward side Scots pines can be seen with their reddish bark often gleaming like fire in the sunlight. From Trow Gill an obvious path leads up to Gaping Gill, and the temptation to approach this too closely should be avoided, as the stream pours over the rim into the hole. This is a truly awesome sight after rain or when the winter snows are melting. On many summer weekends and Bank Holidays it is possible to pay a fee and be winched down in a chair to follow the example of the Frenchman E. A. Martel who in 1895 was the first to descend (using a rope ladder) and return safely. Since then thousands of visitors have made the trip and many report that they feel like steeplejacks working on a cathedral. We prefer to take their word for it and continue upwards to the summit of Ingleborough.

The path is obvious and leads first to Little Ingleborough before climbing onto the main plateau. The flora on the slopes and the summit have been altered over the centuries by the selective grazing of generations of sheep with the hardy Swaledale being particularly common in these parts. On the summit there is a shelter and a view indicator provided by the Fell Rescue Team, the views are spectacular and take in the Cumbrian mountains. Pendle and the Lancashire Pennines and on a clear day, especially in winter, Snaefell on the Isle of Man. We find March and April an ideal time to visit the summit, for here it is still possible to find the attractive cushion-like growth of purple saxifrage.

Those who enjoy their botany should be sure not to miss the walks from Austwick, at one time an important stop on the coach road between Settle and Clapham. Close to the village is a good example of the effect of ice on vegetation. A glacier sweeping down Crummockdale carried erratics from the Wharfe area and deposited glacial drift on the northern face of Oxenbur hill whilst scouring the summit right down to bare rock. Even a superficial glance reveals the startling difference in the flowers of the two regions. On the lower slopes are found acid-loving plants such as sphagnum moss, sundew, cotton grass, bog asphodel and purple moorgrass. On the upper limestone areas the recent shallow coating of soil gives sufficient root space for rock rose, milkwort, harebell, bird's eye primrose and an assortment of helleborines.

All the settlements along the A65 are good centres for those who love walking, and among the most attractive is Ingleton. Here the rivers Twiss and Doe join to form the Greta. A circular walk of around five miles leads up the valley of the Twiss across a patch of open country and then down the Doe Valley, passing a series of cascades and waterfalls on the way. There is a small entrance fee to enter the valleys which are

Lady's slipper orchid.

owned by the Ingleton Scenery Company, but this is well worth it especially for those who like to have their walk wild but well-marked. Steps have been cut through difficult areas, strong wooden bridges cross the streams, and there is even a refreshment hut at the midway point. All this has been achieved without detracting from the savage grandeur of the scene.

There is ample parking at the entrance to the valley walks, but there is another large park around the large information centre in the centre of the village. A steep descent leads to the parish church of St Mary which is a pleasing blend of ancient and modern, standing on the site of a Norman foundation. The thirteenth-century tower still stands but the rest of the building was erected in 1887. The font is Norman, and it is said that during the days of Cromwell's Commonwealth (1649-1660) it was hurled into the river below, only being taken back into the church early in the nineteenth century. The church is usually kept locked but the address of the key holder is prominently displayed and it is worthwhile making the effort if only to see the 'vinegar bible'. This was so named because of a mistake made by a sixteenth-century translator or printer, who confused wine and vinegar!

At the present time Ingleton with its small Friday street market looks as if it has always been 'an olde worlde village' – if there is such a thing – but in the past it was a hive of industrial activity. Coal was mined here for hundreds of years and spinning was also an important industry linked to the wool market at Bradford along a network of busy packhorse routes. Bell Horse Gate in the village is a reminder of these times. After a period of inactivity the mines were reopened in 1913, almost 300 miners were employed, and to house them a redbrick 'model village' was built. The prosperity did not last, however, and the colliery closed for good in 1937.

Ingleton was then obliged to seek out tourists, but this hunt had begun as early as 1849 when the railway arrived from Skipton, and in 1861 an impressively proportioned viaduct was built as part of a link to Sedbergh. Joseph Carr, who is commemorated by a plaque near the church, is given the credit for setting up the Ingleton Improvement Society in 1884. He obtained permission from local landowners to drive a path through the glens and then to extract a fee from the tourists. Part of the money went towards the maintenance of the footpaths and park as compensation to the local folk who suffered some intrusion into their privacy. The scheme worked well then and still works well today.

Heron fishing in the Craven Dales, near Austwick.

Once the Greta has been formed by the union of the Twiss and Doe it travels on to join first the Wenning and then the Lancashire stretch of the Lune close to the village of Hornby.

Both the Twiss and the Doe are substantial streams in their own right – the Twiss receives its waters from Kingsdale and the Doe drains Chapel-le-Dale which itself has a most fascinating history. To the right of the road linking Ingleton and Chapel-le-Dale are the impressive White Scar show caves which are open on most days on payment of a fee. Guided tours are available into the electrically lit interior and there is also an extensive car park plus a cafe and gift shop. This is one of the most impressive limestone caverns in the country, its natural beauty greatly enhanced by the skilful use of coloured lights.

Chapel-le-Dale itself, which once made its money by manufacturing shoes, is dominated by the sheer bulk of the mountains Whernside and Ingleborough. It takes its name from a tiny chapel which, until 1864, was a chapel-of-ease to Ingleton parish church – some locals still call it Ingleton Fells chapel. The Dale was often busy during the turnpike age as horses struggled to pull the coaches up the incline past the well-named Hill Inn. We were surprised to learn from a horse-driving friend that it was just as difficult for the horses to resist the weight of laden coaches on the down slope, and the coachmen often had to pour water on the overheated brakes. This was part of the vital link road between Lancaster and Richmond. Across the road from the inn is the delightful little church which in spring is surrounded by a colourful mass of primroses, violets and wood anemones. Although not visible from the road, the church should not be missed because it has its own fascinating if tragic tale to tell. There is a tablet set into the inner wall which records the names of those who perished during the construction of the Settle to Carlisle railway, and in the churchyard there is an unmarked mass grave in which are buried men, women and children who died of smallpox which struck the shanty town in which the labourers lived. To search for evidence of this shanty town and to see the line they built, the road should be followed past the Hill Inn to Ribblehead, close to the source of the river which gives its name to the next Dale.

CHAPTER 3

Upper Ribblesdale

The best way of exploring Upper Ribblesdale is to use Settle as a base as it is here that the main residential hotels are situated. Settle is on one bank of the River Ribble with Giggleswick on the other, the former having the market centre and the latter the ancient church. Settle is Anglian in origin whilst Giggleswick was a Scandinavian settlement. Following the Norman Conquest when the land was parcelled out among William's followers, the river was an obvious boundary between estates. The Percy family were given Settle but not Giggleswick and by 1249 they had thrived and had been given permission to set up a market each Tuesday. Subsequent owners of Giggleswick do not seem to have fared so well and in 1255 Elias had given away most of his lands to the monks of Fountains Abbey and signed over the remnants to the Percys in exchange for a pension for life.

We have often heard it said that the music of Elgar conjures up the glory of the English countryside, but did not realise how well he knew and loved Settle. The connection between the composer and this lovely limestone region has been well told in a small leaflet called 'The Elgar Way' which can be obtained from the Information Centre in Settle. It all began in 1882 when Dr Charles William Buck from Settle went to a meeting in Worcester of the British Medical Association. Always a keen amateur musician, Dr Buck was asked to play in the Shire Hall as part of an impromptu soirée. The conductor was the then unknown composer Edward Elgar. The two became firm friends and Elgar often travelled by steam train to Settle, played golf on the course which still runs parallel to Giggleswick Scar and walked with Buck on the limestone crags above the town.

We began our own Elgar variation from what is now the National Westminster Bank in Settle's market square. This was once Dr Buck's surgery and there is a plaque on the wall celebrating his friendship with the composer. Whilst staying

The Hoffman Kiln in parts resembles an ancient castle.

here Elgar wrote 'Rosemary' and 'Salut d'amour'. From the old surgery we set off in the direction of Malham intending to visit Scaleber Falls, one of the pair's favourite spots. This passes the increasingly informative Museum of North Craven Life which is open between 2pm and 5pm from July to September except on Mondays when it is closed. From October to Easter it opens only on Saturdays from 2pm to 5pm but it is closed in January and February. Party visits, however, can be made by appointment. There is a small entrance fee and it was here that we discovered that the name Craven is derived from Craig Vaen which means rocky crags, an ideal description for this area and also for that described in the last chapter.

The climb out of Settle is steep but the views of the valley below are spectacular and worth the strenuous climb to Scaleber, a distance of just over one mile from Settle. It is, however, possible to reach Scaleber Force by car and there is limited parking close to the cascade. Water tumbles over 40 feet (13 metres) of stepped cliffs and spray is bounced into the wooded dell which is so moist that it is the perfect habitat for liverworts and mosses as well as flowering plants such as golden saxifrage and wood sorrel. This idyllic spot, cool in summer and sheltered in winter, was loved by Elgar and he even had a photograph of Scaleber in his study, probably a gift from Dr Buck. In the meadow land on the Settle side of the fall as the beck descends to meet the Ribble, flowers grow well, especially lady's smock or cuckoo flower and self heal. This is also cuckoo country and on one memorable June day we picnicked here after watching a huge young cuckoo being fed by a pair of diminutive meadow pipits. In some of the streamlets the little blue flowers of brooklime are found between May and September, whilst watercress is abundant in the clear unpolluted water. All this scenery cannot have failed to attract the busy doctor and ambitious musician. It must have relaxed the former and inspired the latter.

The Settle air had its effect upon other famous folk, as a walk around the town quickly proves. The Trustee Savings Bank bears a plaque commemorating the fact that on this site was born on February 20th 1839 the Rev. Benjamin Waugh, known as the Children's Friend. He was the founder of the Society for the Prevention of Cruelty to Children. In Giggleswick church, to which we shall return later, is a memorial to the memory of George Birkbeck, the founder of the Mechanics' Institutes and also London's Birkbeck College. The Birkbecks were one of the main shareholders in the Craven Bank which opened in 1791 to meet a need created by the increasingly busy turnpike roads. The prosperity of any town depends upon the efficiency of its communications system. In 1753 the Keighley to Kendal turnpike was constructed at low level, thus avoiding the steep route from Long Preston via Hunter Bank and Upper Settle. Just outside Settle on the road to Long Preston is a toll house built during this period, and now that the town has been bypassed it is possible to examine this without risk to life or limb. The Golden Lion in Settle is a good example of what a coaching inn was like, the stables are still present and their atmosphere survives because they are still used by horses. Occasionally, particularly for weddings, a coach and four rattles out of the yard and all Settle finds time to stop and stare. The original arched entrance has long been demolished but another can be seen on the opposite side of the road.

As on all other routes, the coming of the railway proved to be the deathknell of the turnpikes and a track was laid to Settle and Giggleswick as early as 1840. Settle was commercially much more important than Giggleswick and it was about this time that its residents gained permission to erect their own parish church. It is a rather plain structure, now opposite the large car park, dominated by towering railway arches and would not be worth a visit if it did not contain a tribute to an engineering legend. Inside the entrance is a plaque 'To the memory of those who, through accident, lost their lives in constructing the railway works between Settle and Dent Head'. This tablet was erected at the joint expense of their fellow workmen and the Midland Railway Company. The Midland first planned the Settle to Carlisle link to provide an alternative route into Scotland, and even some experienced engineers thought the terrain far too difficult, especially around Ribblehead, and that the scheme was ill-advised. The line, which opened for traffic in 1876, came under threat throughout the 1980s, but several times proved its worth when either the east- or west-coast routes had problems. The Settle to Carlisle is then a remedial option allowing transfer of traffic between the two main routes but it was its tourist potential which finally saved it. The steam-hauled excursions are booked up weeks ahead and enthusiasts line every bridge and cameras click like machine guns as the old but beautifully restored engines climb through some of the finest scenery in the country.

Before following the line up Ribblesdale some time should be allowed to explore Giggleswick and Settle, one of the best views being from the summit of Castleburg, a hill bearing a flagpole which is signposted from Settle market place, itself dominated by the Shambles, a row of buildings overlooking the cross. Originally this was just a simple row of two-storey cottages with the butchers slaughtering their cattle on one level with other sections being occupied by blacksmiths, wheelwrights and the like. In Victorian times a third storey was added to give the Shambles a dignified appearance not at all related to its original function. Another building which should not be missed is known as 'Preston's Folly', constructed in 1679 and looking like a most splendid Jacobean residence. All is not quite what it

The Hoffman Kiln – could it become a museum?

seems, however, as once the front was complete Preston had no cash left to spend on the interior. All that was constructed here was a magnificent staircase which does much to enhance the displays laid out by the owner of the antique shop now housed in poor old Preston's Folly.

Parking is not easy in Giggleswick but it is worth the trouble to walk over the Ribble Bridge from Settle and descend the winding street to the grand old church of St Alkelda, a Saxon woman killed for her Christian faith by the Danes. Only two churches are dedicated to her memory, the other being at Middleham in Wensleydale described in Chapter 6. Some scholars wonder if the lady may be something of a myth and suggest that the name may derive from the old English 'haeligkeld' which means the holy well. When the church was being restored towards the end of last century a most remarkable discovery was made: buried with Sir Richard

Tempest, a fifteenth-century knight, was his beloved war horse!

The village is dominated by the green oxidised copper dome of Giggleswick school chapel. One of Britain's oldest and most distinguished establishments founded in 1547 by James Carr, Giggleswick was substantially improved in 1552 by John Nowell the vicar of St Alkelda's. Many old scholars distinguished themselves in later life including Dr Abraham Sutcliffe, who is said to have introduced the mangel-worzel into Britain and has been blessed by farmers ever since. George Birkbeck was also educated here and a more recent success was the late Russell Harty who taught at Giggleswick in the 1960s before becoming a TV presenter.

On the side of the road climbing alongside Giggleswick Scar is the famous Ebbing and Flowing Well, much more easily observed these days since the Settle bypass was constructed and reduced the traffic. The well is fed by a spring and as it fills up the weight of water presses an underground plug and the well suddenly drains. There is a local tale – we don't care if it is true or not – of a traveller long ago allowing his horse to slake its thirst. The animal began to drink just as the well emptied and the astonished man took his horse back to Settle to find out from the local ostler whether or not the beast would burst!

From Settle the route into Upper Ribblesdale passes close to Langcliffe, meaning the long cliff, a village mentioned in the Domesday survey; it was one of the areas given by Elias of Giggleswick to monastic institutions; this time the Cistercians of Sawley were the recipients. This is great walking country and one long trek leads back into Settle via Scaleber, yet another route well known to Elgar and Buck. One of our favourites is to Victoria Cave, a good walk in all seasons, but we prefer it in winter. We remember one day when snowdrifts reflected the bright sunshine and the views of Ingleborough and Penyghent were wonderfully clear. Up on the hill a farmer struggled through the snow on his tractor carrying fodder to his sheep, his dog having an easy day riding on the passenger seat, well knowing that hungry sheep do not need to be gathered. Down below in the valley the fields looked green and lush in sharp contrast to the ice-age conditions we had to contend with on the heights. A sharp climb through even deeper, crisper snow

Knapweed was once known as 'loggerheads'.

led to Victoria Cave, originally discovered in 1838 and named after the Queen who was crowned in that year, after her ascent of the throne the year before. All that can be seen today is a massive cave with no tourist trappings whatever, but this seems to add to its atmosphere. Many bones were found here including those of the long-extinct straight-tusked elephant and slender-nosed rhinoceros as well as those of wild horse, oxen and hyena. Human bones and coins relating to the Romano-British period were also discovered along with fish hooks, brooches and silver necklaces. These cave dwellers seem to have led a surprisingly sophisticated life and we feel it is a pity that most of the artefacts are now housed in the British Museum and too few are displayed in the Museum of Craven Life down in Settle. Langcliffe village also has a goodly share of more recent history; it initially lacked a parish church but the old footpath down to Giggleswick can still be followed over much of its route. Langcliffe might well have developed into a settlement to rival Settle but for a disastrous raid by the Scots in 1318 which totally destroyed the village so that a newer and much poorer hamlet was built about half a mile to the south. An excavation of the old village site, we are sure, would be well worth the effort. Some link with this can perhaps be seen at Cross Green in the present village which was once an inn and still has the sign of a naked woman embedded in the wall. There is also a 'Naked Man' in Settle market place, not now an inn but a cafe. The two figures have been linked by some antiquaries but they have not quite managed to convince serious historians with their theories. They suggest that the pair may have been part of some nature-based pagan religion usurped by Christianity and perhaps practised in the ancient village of Langcliffe.

We cannot even trust the datestone over the porch of Langcliffe Hall which reads 1602 and was probably incorporated into the present building, possibly the third on the present site, from an earlier structure. Two brothers of the Paley family of Langcliffe fought the Scots at Flodden in 1513 and perhaps got some revenge for the destruction of the old village. It is the Dawsons, however, who have dominated the more recent history of the village, Isaac Newton (1642-1727) was a friend of William Dawson and it is said that he may have been the first to read *Principia*, the work which established the great man's reputation. There was a time between 1912 and 1919 and again from 1921 to 1941, periods including the two world wars, when Langcliffe was often kept directly informed of the great news stories. Geoffrey Dawson was the editor of *The Times* during these momentous days and spent much time with his aunt at Langcliffe Hall. The old lady would not install a telephone and so Geoffrey kept in touch with his office via messages relayed from Settle railway station.

The village also had its share of industry and it was this which in 1851 led to Hector Christie, cotton manufacturer, constructing a church and instructing his workers, many from Cornish Wesleyan stock, to worship here rather than in their own chapel. Cotton is not a part of the modern economy, but the 1868 mill still stands and is used to process waste paper, but

One of the many delightful tracks running through Crummackdale.

a stroll by the river reveals all the weirs and sluices which once provided reliable supplies of water for the boilers. Nearby is another example of an extinct industry – the Hoffman Kiln, a unique example of lime-burning on a large scale. There have been several efforts during the early 1990s to establish the crumbling structure as an information and visitor centre, but raising the capital required has proved an obstacle. The idea was to establish a museum of quarrying and mining and to feed it a stream of tourists via the Settle to Carlisle railway. The kiln during its working life had its own substantial sidings off the main railway. Built to a German design, it is a circular brick structure 150 feet (46 metres) in circumference with sixteen burning chambers which could be stoked and raked by workers moving in a circle. Lime-burning thrived until other chemicals were developed, but in its day the Ribblesdale Hoffman supplied blast furnaces, tanning and building works and also 'whitewash factories'. Lime is still used in the manufacture of paper, paint, glass and even in sugar refineries although techniques from its production are much more sophisticated than in the days of the Hoffman. We still hope that the museum idea can be realised.

In the meantime the kiln has been taken over by nature. A disused nearby quarry, now a municipal rubbish tip, is the haunt of gulls and jackdaws whilst the kiln and its surroundings are overgrown with flowers. Prominent species include marjoram and knapweed. The latter has purple flowers which when they die down have hard fruits which were once rubbed like teasels over cloth to raise the nap and thus earn the flower its name. It was also once known as loggerheads because of the round head on top of a thin stem. A loggerhead was a medieval weapon made up of an iron ball mounted on a wooden handle. Protagonists struck out with this dangerous weapon and this is what is meant when we say we are at loggerheads with someone.

Further up the dale around Helwith Bridge the quarrying of limestone is still a vital industry, but between this unsightly area and Langcliffe is a touch of gentle old England at Stainforth. Actually the village is split in two by the Ribble, the main settlement and car park being at Friars Stainforth with Knights Stainforth sited close to the river. Originally the name was Stainford meaning stepping stones over a ford. Knights Stainford Hall, now a farmhouse, is a splendid Tudor dwelling which once belonged to the Tempest family and then to the D'Arcys. Samuel Watson restored the house and also provided a packhorse bridge over the Ribble around 1670 which has been in the care of the National Trust since 1931. Its steepness and narrowness create something of a traffic hazard but fortunately there is a better route in from Giggleswick. In an area sadly lacking in tourist facilities Knights Stainford Hall farm has a well-appointed caravan site, and if there is a better place for touring vans in the Dales, then we have failed to find it.

Close to Stainforth Force, a popular spot with anglers, is Stackhouses where there are the remains of an old fish pass which may have belonged to Furness Abbey and which was designed to prevent fish being washed downstream whilst allowing the strong migratory fish such as salmon to move upstream to the spawning grounds. The Ribble has long been an important source of food. Stackhouse Hall was the home of John Carr, the founder of Giggleswick school.

Above the main river and on the opposite side of the road and railway line is Friars Stainforth which once belonged to the monks of Salley (or Sawley) Abbey near Clitheroe. Cowside

Penyghent – one of the most delightful of Yorkshire's mountains, best climbed from Horton-in-Ribblesdale. This view is from the opposite side.

Beck, which drains the west side of Malham Moor, is spanned by a modern but attractive bridge, but few visitors can resist crossing the ancient stepping stones which gave the settlement its name. These and the packhorse bridge over the Ribble were on the old route from Lancaster to York.

Just beyond the Stainforths, Upper Ribblesdale suddenly shows signs of its still essential industrial function with a series of quarries, some long since deserted but others still working at full blast – literally. Helwith Bridge is connected to Austwick via a delightfully unspoiled road which passes close to the remote village of Wharfe and the track leading up through Crummockdale which is one of the area's undiscovered byways. Crummockdale is criss-crossed by tiny streams and flat stone bridges and is a paradise for walkers of all standards. We once had the pleasure of travelling this route by horse-drawn caravan, following the route taken by a family of travellers on their way to the June horse fair at Appleby in Cumbria.

Gone are the days of small-scale quarry blasting with unskilled workers hoping that they could blast out a few tons of the rock fare and avoid injury. These days a computer-controlled explosion brings down many thousands of tons of stone with sufficient built-in safety measures to ensure security.

41

Likewise the fallen rock is removed and treated using the very latest technology. It is the sheer volume of a hillside which can be removed which worries conservationists, and yet what is the answer to the insatiable demand for this material? Tarmac Roadstone and the Dry Rigg quarry of Redland Aggregates produce slate and greywacke, a sedimentary rock laid down between 570 and 280 million years ago. This is a complex mixture of sandstone, feldspar and some ferromagnesian compounds. When crushed, this material results in a great variety of grain sizes, which when laid on roads and particularly airport runways prevents skidding. It is therefore a vital material. What, you may ask, happened to the limestone? To discover the answer to a visit to the disused Arcow quarry between the two modern workings is needed. Because of its geological interest Arcow has been declared an S.S.S.I. (Site of Special Scientific Interest), and here is a beautiful example of an Unconformity. Younger carboniferous limestones lie on the eroded surface of the greywackes which are steeply inclined. The junction – or Unconformity – illustrates a geological time gap of several million years, and once more we find examples of changes in flora as we move from one stratum to another.

By the time Horton-in-Ribblesdale is reached the effects of heavy industry are almost forgotten and here is a village of pubs and cafes catering for the healthy appetites of fell walkers. From close to the splendid old church there is a choice of routes up to the 2273-feet (692,5 metre) summit of Penyghent. The path is obvious, the climb relatively gentle, and on the summit grow cushions of purple saxifrage and also cloudberries, whilst among the breeding birds are ring ousels and golden plovers whose plaintive whistles are so much a feature of a springtime walk. The church dates from the reign of Henry I (1100-1135) and it was initially controlled by the monks of Jervaulx Abbey in Wensleydale, although by 1249 it had passed via the Archbishop of York to the nuns of Clemmenthorpe. Quite a lot of the early Norman work remains although substantial additions were made in the fourteenth and fifteenth centuries. At the time of the Reformation a fine piece of stained glass of the coat of arms of Jervaulx and also the mitred head of Thomas à Becket were brought to Horton and installed in the west window.

The Viaduct at Ribblehead.

We once sat in the bar of the Crown Inn discussing – literally – the ups and downs of life with two parties of university students. One group had just descended from Ingleborough and were about to tackle Penyghent, whilst the second group, satisfied that it was not going to rain, were preparing to descend into Alum Pot. This is one of the most famous pot holes in the Dales and is reached from Selside and is 198 feet (60.3 metres) deep. They told us that it was first described by the clergyman John Hutton in his book *A Tour of The Caves* published in 1781; the next recorded descent was made in 1847 by two local lads, John Birkbeck and William Metcalf. They were all agreed that the stalactite and stalagmite formations were no better than those found in other systems including the showcaves, but the attraction to pot holers is the sheer size of the chambers, especially the Long Churn beyond which is a 60-foot (18.3 metre) underground waterfall. There are other minor pot holes near the village including Hull Pot to the east, whilst the whole area is dotted with drumlins (see page 2).

These days the village of Selside looks dark, but this is because it is overshadowed by the huge railway embankment. Its name derives from the Norse Saether meaning a sheep enclosure and it was used as such by the monks of Furness Abbey. Colt Park was also a Furness farm, this time to graze their horses, and its woodland is now a nature reserve (permit required), being one of the finest examples of a limestone woodland in Britain. Birds eye primrose, globe flower,

43

The golden plover is a breeding bird of Upper Ribblesdale.

baneberry and several species of orchid grow here. Opposite the wood is Lodge Hall farm which was one of the Granges (or farms) belonging to the Cistercian monks of Furness.

In addition to the natural beauty, anyone interested in the history and engineering problems associated with the Railway Age should allow plenty of time to explore the area between Selside and Ribblehead and study a large-scale OS map very closely. There is a good caravan site at Selside and it is close to the Mouth of Hell, otherwise known as Alum Pot. Water from the pot resurfaces at Tarn Dub near Newhouses. Also near Selside is Ling Gill, a nature reserve administered by the Nature Conservancy which supports a varied limestone flora. There are some deep and potentially dangerous shafts known as the Calf Holes. A permit from the Conservancy at Merlewood, Grange-over-Sands, Cumbria is required.

A small group of houses called Salt Lake City indicates that American Mormon workmen were employed during the construction of the Ribblehead viaduct, one of the most photographed sections of the Settle-Carlisle railway. Ribblehead itself is not even a village any more – although there was a shanty town here during the railway days – but merely a junction of roads between Ingleton, Settle and Hawes. As the T-junction is approached, the traveller is faced by the 2,414-foot (745-metre) bulk of Whernside, the least known of the three peaks. The summit is about three miles from Ribblehead but it is a tough walk, although one loved by naturalists, for here are small tarns around which black-headed gulls breed, and the heathery slopes are also the haunt of cuckoo, wheatear, red grouse, lapwing and golden plover. Whernside is always breezy and in high wind can be positively dangerous: there are records of gales actually stopping trains crossing the Ribblehead viaduct. This is 1328 feet (405 metres) long, 105 feet (32 metres) high and has 24 arches. It deserves to be preserved as a national monument, and this now looks more likely as the Settle-Carlisle railway has become such a tourist attraction. All that is left at Ribblehead is the Station Inn and the railway halt itself which, although wind-damaged, still retains its platforms and dilapidated waiting room.

The Ribble rises in the mossy, peaty uplands around Ribblehead and not far from the source of the Wharfe and the Ure which flow eastwards before reaching the coast via the Humber. This area is truly one of the great watersheds of England.

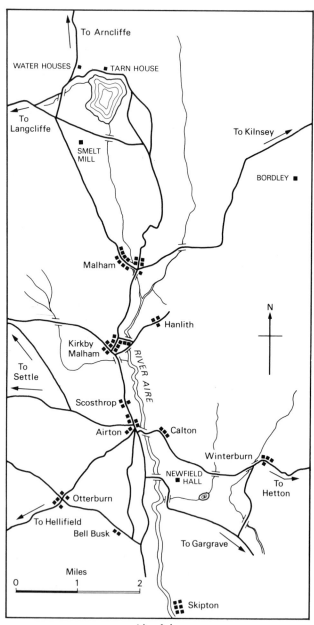

To Arncliffe

WATER HOUSES ■ TARN HOUSE

To Langcliffe

SMELT MILL

To Kilnsey

BORDLEY ■

Malham

Hanlith

Kirkby Malham

RIVER AIRE

To Settle

Scosthrop

Airton

Calton

Winterburn

NEWFIELD HALL

To Hetton

Otterburn

To Hellifield

Bell Busk

To Gargrave

N

Miles
0   1   2

Skipton

Airedale.

CHAPTER 4

Malham and Airedale

When we first began to explore the Yorkshire Dales we had some difficulty in distinguishing Malhamdale and Airedale. Where was the river Malham? Slowly, and armed with our Ordnance Survey map, we discovered the source of the Aire close to Malham village, that there was no River Malham and that Upper Airedale was in fact called Malhamdale. The parish of Kirkby Malham stretches eleven miles from Bell Busk in the south to the breezy Malham Moor in the north. It controls the ecclesiastical life of Calton, Otterburn, Airton, Scotshrop, Hanlith and Malham itself as well as Kirkby Malham, the site of the magnificent church.

Malham Tarn is the highest stretch of freshwater in the Pennines, being 1230 feet (375 metres) above sea level, with a maximum depth of only around 13 feet (4 metres). This means that its 150 acres (60 hectares) provide rich, reed-fringed bays ideal for feeding wildfowl although its very shallowness makes it liable to freeze over during really cold spells. The nature trail around the tarn has been carefully designed to provide good views of the birds which include pochard, goosander, tufted duck, teal and the ubiquitous mallard and teal. On one magnificently clear February morning we watched sixty whooper swans and red-throated diver reflected in the calm waters under a cold blue sky. The tarn and the house which overlooks it are now run as a residential field studies centre by the Nature Conservancy Council under lease since 1948 from the National Trust. Amateur naturalists make up the bulk of the students. The trails are always open and a leaflet can be obtained from an honesty box at the start of the well-signposted route. It is no wonder that geology features heavily in the courses on offer, because the tarn itself has a history which has proved difficult to unravel. Set as it is in the middle of a limestone area which is naturally porous, why does the tarn not 'leak'? During the period following the ice ages large amounts of muddy clay and gravel debris were deposited in the shallow depression forming an efficient natural plug. This material is called glacial moraine. Because of the surrounding limestone moorland Malham Tarn water is hard, thus providing chemicals essential for invertebrates to build up their skeletons, and these form the base for a food chain supporting a good population of fish and birds. No wonder the monks of Fountains Abbey had a successful fish farm at Malham. The tarn was given to the monks in the twelfth century by the Norman, William de Percy who in turn had received it from William the Conqueror who had taken it from the Saxons.

Following the dissolution of the abbeys around 1540 Malham was purchased by the Clifford family, but by 1780 Lord Ribblesdale owned the estate and set about producing an extensive shooting and woodland complex. The effect of this can still be seen today in the great variety of woodland birds including jay, great spotted and green woodpecker plus moorland species such as red grouse, lapwing, golden plover, while in summer wheatears breed amongst the rocks. He also dammed the tarn and raised its level slightly. The Ribblesdales, however, did not stay long and in 1852 James Morrison bought Malham and constructed a fine house above the tarn and screened it with trees. His son Walter remained a bachelor and Malham House became famous for its distinguished literary and scientific guests including Charles Darwin, John Ruskin, John Stuart Mill and the then famous Lord Avebury, the foremost botanist of his age. Walter's library was one of the best in private hands and he specialised in local history and folklore. The present field centre has thus a more impressive pedigree of learning than the majority of similar establishments. Two other guests were Thomas Hughes, the author of *Tom Brown's Schooldays'*, and the Rev. Charles Kingsley (1819-1875) who spent much of his life in the Yorkshire Dales and whose *Water Babies*, published in 1863, is something of a Malhamdale saga. There is a description of young Tom the chimney sweep escaping from his master by scrambling down Malham Cove, and the dark scratches on the wall of the cove were said to have been caused by his dirty finger nails. Walter Morrison was a benefactor of his old school at Giggleswick in Ribblesdale and contributed the then huge figure of £50,000 to construct the chapel whose green copper

Aire Springs. The river's source is among the pebbles between Malham and Kirkby Malham.

dome is a local landmark. He tended to give anonymously, but was not a true recluse since he was a Liberal Member of Parliament for more than forty years.

Concentrating on fact rather than fiction, Kinglsey described the cove as "The awful cliff filling up the valley with a sheer cross wall, and from beneath a black lip at the foot, the whole

River Aire coming up clear as crystal from unknown abysses."

We now know that this account of the source of the Aire is not correct but it is quite a reasonable assumption as the stream emerging from the tarn disappears as though down a plug hole into the Water Sinks, emerging at the foot of Malham Cove which is 325 feet (100 metres) high and 975 feet (300 metres) wide, at which point it is known as Malham Beck. By placing dyes in the water it now seems that the stream going down the Water Sinks appears again are Aire Springs. The cove water has been found to originate about a mile to the west of the tarn close to an old lead-smelting mill. Some goelogists feel that both theories may be correct, especially after heavy rain when a degree of mixing may occur in the tortuous bowels of the earth so very typical of limestone areas. Between the village and the cove the road and footpath follow Malham Beck and from it there are panoramic views of limestone hills, especially Cawden which bisects the view. There are views especially in winter when the low sun throws shadows on the hillsides, revealing lynchets – terraces dug into the hillside to make cultivation easier – which were typical of the farming techniques of the Celtic and later civilisations.

Another path leads first to Gordale Scar and then on to join Mastiles Lane, an ancient trackway to Kilnsey in Wharfedale. It is just possible to park close to Gordale Scar but it is much more rewarding to walk the steep path for just over a mile following the line of Gordale Beck, via Janet's Foss. This is not a high fall, but is one of the most attractive in the Dales, the water being so hard that yellowish deposits of tufa – looking like fur in a kettle – are found along the banks and around the fall itself. Gordale Scar was once a huge cave, and what we see today is the result of a tremendous roof fall, the scene having changed little since the Rev. John Hutton wrote in his *Tour of the Caves* in 1780 that 'Some goats frisked about with seemingly wanton carelessness, on the brink of this dreadful precipice, where none of us would have stood for all the pleasant vales washed by the river Aire.'

In the early days of tourism, recorded faithfully by Hutton, upland scenery was regarded as frightening, the lush lowland greenery being preferred. This is reflected in James Ward's painting completed in 1815 and now exhibited in the Tate

Bill Wild's stainless steel kingfisher in Kirkby Malham Church.

Gallery. The Scar is depicted with great accuracy but he then adds a couple of touches of artistic licence in the form of a herd of cattle plus a white bull and a couple of battling red deer stags. The work was completed for Thomas, Lord Lister, which accounts for the Chillingham-type white cattle, a herd of which the patron once kept in Gisburne Park. Modern country lovers do not mind high hills and soaring cliffs and Gordale is now climbed along a steep winding path up onto Malham Moor. They enjoy watching kestrels and pigeons breeding on the ledges and listening to the larks soaring above.

The village area itself has been occupied since the Bronze Age and is now one of the tourist traps of the Dales with its Visitor Centre usually crowded with school parties and walkers. But Malham was once a site of industry with a cotton mill, tan pits, calamine and copper mines on Pikedaw, lead mining and smelting on the moor, and coal mining on Fountains Fell. Much of the material was taken downdale to Gargrave, especially after the Leeds to Liverpool Canal came into operation at the turn of the nineteenth century. Industry did not eliminate the atmosphere of the eighth-century Anglian settlement, nor has the recent growth of tourism. The results of medieval religious competition can still be seen in and around the village. Land to the west of Malham Beck was controlled by the Cistercian monks of Fountains, whilst to the east the land was controlled by the Augustinian canons of Bolton Priory in Wharfedale. Between the village and Malham Cove is a stone clapper bridge named after Prior Moon of Bolton. Priors Hall farm is on the site of Bolton's local administrative centre and Malham Hall was the local base for the business enterprises of Fountains Abbey. Beck Hall, also on the site of a buiding belonging to Fountains, later became a dower house belonging to Malham Tarn House. With all these monastic lands it is not surprising to find that whatever other industries were developed, sheep farming played a very important role, as it still does. Given this religious history, many casual visitors wonder why there is no parish church.

To discover this we must follow the infant Aire downstream to Kirkby Malham. The name derives from the Sandinavian 'church close to Malham'. It does seem to be a large chuch for such a small village but it is the mother church for a huge parish which once came under the influence of yet another abbey. In 1199 Adam 'the son of Adam of Giggleswick' purged his soul by giving Malhamdale lands to the Premonstratensian White Canons of St Mary at West Dereham in Norfolk. Until the Reformation the canons appointed the vicars. Although the substantial church was restored in 1879, a great many fifteenth and sixteenth-century features remain, and the millstone grit tower around 70 feet (21 metres) high was built in 1490. The interior of the church is of great interest to the historian, especially the memorial to John Lambert from nearby Calton,

The supports of the stocks and the Squatter's House on the Green at Airton.

who became one of Cromwell's most reliable generals. This connection accounts for Oliver Cromwell's signature on three marriage certificates which have to be kept out of reach of 'over-ambitious collectors'. Some historians have expressed doubts about the validity of the signatures, but we have seen them and fail to see any reason why anyone should have bothered to forge such a document, especially in the days after the Commonwealth when the former dictator was anything but popular. Among the furniture are a number of thirteenth-century gravestones, a fifteenth-century muniment and vestment chest, a set of box pews installed between 1631 and 1723 and a trio of bells with the huge tenor dated 1601 and weighing 25 cwt. More recent pieces include a steel engraving commemorating the life of the eighteenth-century explorer Captain James King who went with Captain Cook to the South Seas. Our favourite artefact is a lovely stainless steel carving of a kingfisher by Bill Wild, the local blacksmith and artist. Locals who remember Bill at prayer have, since his death, been able to enjoy the sight of his kingfisher now secured to the window ledge.

If you ever wonder what a watery grave looks like, then you

need look no further than the churchyard at Kirkby Malham. Here are buried Colonel John Harrison and his wife Helen, the two being often separated, but they obviously retained their sense of humour. A little stream runs down the centre of the grave of Helen who died in 1890 and John who followed in 1900, and they are separated in death by the water which had also separated the soldier on active service abroad from his beloved. Also in the churchyard are the stocks situated just inside the lych gates, and a right turn away from the main road leads to the old vicarage, once a hall restored in 1620 before serving as a workhouse and then as a cotton mill. There was also a bobbin mill in the area and another cotton mill at Scargill which was once the manorial corn mill on the way to Hanlith which means "the hillslope owned by Hagena". Even today the settlement is tiny and dominated almost entirely by an attractive seventeenth-century hall, with its doorway carrying the initials "RS 1668" – after Robert Sarjeanson. The presence of halberds engraved on either side of the door is significant and tells us that the Sarjeansons were an influential family. A halberd was a lethal hybrid between a battle axe and a spear and could only be portrayed on houses of those who provided valuable military service to their lord.

Hanlith is somewhat remote from the tourist areas and the same applies to Airton, but the network of footpaths around each provide some of the most attractive and underrated walking in the Dales. Few walks can rival the stroll along the Aire upstream from Airton to Malham or downstream to Gargrave. Airton is an old Quaker village – the name of which derives from the Saxon meaning a settlement on the Aire. The name of the nearby hamlet of Scotsthrop denotes the colonisation by the Danes by way of Scotland and there must have been a great deal of intermingling of cultures around this area. The only building of note here is the seventeenth-century manor house, but who cares when there is still so much peace to be had for free? Airton's peaceful atmosphere emanates from its central green. There is no pub here, the central position being occupied by what is known as the squatter's house which is surrounded by a walled garden This is a reminder of the times when anyone could lay claim to land on which he managed, during a 24-hour period, to construct a

The pigeon loft at Airton was once an important source of food.

dwelling and have smoke coming out of the chimney – or perhaps in those days a hole in the roof. The stone supports of the stocks are also a reminder of the days of isolation when each village dealt with its own law breakers. There is a Quaker burial ground behind the old Meeting House and almost opposite this is the house built by Quakers William and Alice Ellis in 1696. This has pigeon holes high in the eaves, guaranteeing the owners a supply of young birds which were killed before they were able to fly. These 'larders' were carefully farmed to ensure that the parents kept enough of their offspring to prevent them from deserting the site. The Quakers were hard working and the Ellis's were no exception, their textile mill – first linen and then cotton – having since been converted to flats after a period in the hands of Reckitt and Colman who produced Dettol here. No doubt some of the product 'disinfected' the river, which has long since recovered.

Airton is one of our favourite spots in the Dales, with ideal picnic spots close to the bridge beneath which are an interesting collection of masons' marks. A pleasant stroll leads to the hamlet of Calton, reached via a short cul-de-sac off the road to Winterburn. This is named after a small stream usually only evident after winter rains. Here is Friar Head House built in the seventeenth century from stone of an earlier dwelling which once belonged to the mighty abbey of Furness, yet another monastery with extensive lands in the Dales. Sir Stephen Procter was born at Friars Head and it may well have been this which inspired him to build Fountains Hall, now set at the entrance to the ruins of the Cistercian abbey. Winterburn church was built as an Independent Meeting House in 1704, one of the earliest centres for Congregational worship in the country. Support was given by Barbara, the wife of John Lambert the son of Cromwell's major-general, and a lady of strong religious beliefs. Local legend tells of a burial ground and a sealed-up dungeon from which the tortured cries of an imprisoned monk are occassionally heard by the superstitious.

Calton, however, provides us with some solid fact instead of fable, for Calton Hall was the home of Major-General John Lambert the Parliamentarian; following the Restoration of Charles II in 1660 the Hall was badly damaged by fire, and although no culprits were ever brought to justice, it appears to have been an act of revenge. Lambert, however, was not a cruel enemy and Cromwell gave him the title of 'Honest John', a reputation he had earned during the capture of Bradford. He died in prison in the Channel Islands but in 1688 his son, also called John had the Hall and lands restored to him. The son rebuilt his father's Hall and the history of the soldier is recorded on a plaque set into a gatepost, although the house is not open to the public.

The Airdale explorer may travel by car or along a riverside footpath to Gargrave. Although a tourist village, this once was a market town now sandwiched between the Aire and the Leeds to Liverpool Canal. Once the central parish of Craven, St Andrew's Church is of ancient foundation, and Whittaker thought that stones from a Roman fort were incorporated into the tower when it was built in 1521. There is evidence of at least two earlier churches on the site, confirmed by fragments of Anglian crosses brought inside to protect them from the weather. Alas, all that remains of the 1521 church is the tower, the rest of the building dating to 1851. Nothing remains today to remind us of the Roman presence, and the same is true of

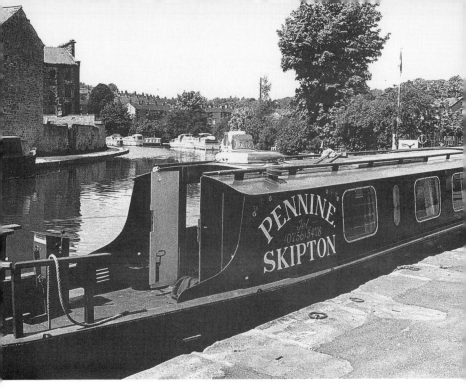

Pleasure craft on the Springs branch of the Leeds to Liverpool Canal.

the monks from Sawley Abbey in Ribbledale who had so much influence on Gargrave between the twelfth and the middle of the sixteenth centuries.

Our favourite walk begins at St Andrew's Church and follows the Aire downstream before crossing a fine set of stepping stones overlooked by cottages to a paved path leading into the village. From the stepping stones Johnson's factory can be seen, and this is the major employer in the area. The company makes baby powder and sterile dressings, the Gargrave plant being concerned with the latter.

The main street has several good tea shops and cafes and a winding road leads to a set of locks on the Leeds to Liverpool Canal. Gargrave was on the turnpike road (now the A65) between Keighley and Kendal and there are a number of old coaching inns and a toll-house cottage on the outskirts of the village on the Skipton side. When the canal opened in the late eighteenth century it reduced the price of coal amost by half and packet boats were soon carrying passengers much more smoothly and cheaply than by coach. Gargrave also served as the focus for the lead miners of Malham whose metal could then be sent to the developing towns at competitive prices. It is truly amazing to see how well the wildlife has adapted to the canal, and we once watched a family of mallards enter the lock at Gargrave to be lifted along with the narrowboat to the upper pound on the canal. The pound is the stretch of level water between the locks.

From Gargrave the Aire flows on to Skipton, a delightful market town and an ideal centre for the exploration of Airedale, Wharfedale and the Craven district. Skipton marks the end of the part of Airedale that is in the Dales, and those who want to follow the river should travel on through Kildwick to Keighley, past Kirkstall Abbey and into Leeds. The river, now very much industrialised, flows on close to the grounds of Temple Newsam before merging with the Ouse near Airmyn.

The first place that should be visited in Skipton is the Museum of Craven Life, housed adjacent to the Town hall. Here is a display of geological and historical artefacts including a splendid collection of photographs of the Leeds to Liverpool Canal in the late 1800s. Skipton's charter was granted in 1203, market day being Monday. It held an important position at the crossing first of green roads and then during the days of packhorse and turnpike routes, and development was aided by the close proximity of the canal. Whilst the main line of the canal skirts around Skipton, a substantial cut called the Springs Branch was built to feed into the very centre of the town. This mini-project was suggested to the advisors of young Lord Thanet of Skipton Castle, and the Springs Branch served not only the town but also ended below the face of his limestone quarries close to the castle walls. A loading chute led down to a small and now disused wharf, but the stretch in the town centre is now a colourful haven of activity and adds yet one more tourist attraction. Another popular attraction is the finely proportioned Norman castle which, despite a great deal of subsequent building, has retained much of its original plan. The original gateway sandwiched between two round towers is singularly attractive, as is the central courtyard around which the castle was constructed. This area is made even darker by the presence of an ancient yew tree. Although the original castle was constructed by Robert de Romilli in the twelfth

A restored toll house at Skipton.

century, we know that by 1311 the vast estates were under the control of the Clifford family, and this continued until the death of Lady Anne Clifford in 1676. In 1323 the area of Skipton – (Anglo-Saxon for sheep-town) was a jigsaw of pasture bounded by huge tracts of forest, and marshy meadows along the flood plains of the Wharfe and the Aire. The male Cliffords, with one notable exception, were warlords rather than farmers and six of them died in battle before they reached the age of forty. 'Butcher Clifford' was the most bloodthirsty and he apparently murdered the Earl of Rutland whom he had captured in battle during the Wars of the Roses. He also discovered the son of the Duke of York in the rear of the defeated army after the Battle of Wakefield in 1460, and remembering that the Duke had killed his own father, he hacked the child to death whilst shouting 'As thy father killed mine so I will kill thee'. He then searched the battlefield until he found the Duke's corpse, hacked off the head and paraded it before the distraught Duchess with the words 'Madam, your war is done. I bring thee a King's ransom'. He then impaled the head on Mickelgate Bar in York.

Atrocities were committed on both sides, and when the Lancastrian Butcher himself fell in battle at Dittondale near Castleford in 1461, the white rose butchers went in search of his son, the eight-year-old Henry Clifford. Friends spirited the child away to the hills of Cumberland where he tended sheep until Richrd III perished at Boswell and in 1485 the youngster could safely return to Skipton, from which time on he was known as the Shepherd Lord. Although his childhood may have been peaceful, he was true to his breeding when it came to a battle and in 1513 at the age of 60 he led a band of his retainers who fought at Flodden against the Scots. On his death in 1523 Henry, the Shepherd's son, was made Earl of Cumberland as a tribute to his father. The new Earl was a good businessman who looked after Skipton Castle and on the dissolution of the abbeys acquired much of Bolton Priory's lands. He was, apparently, a friend of the monks and may well have treated the brethren with more consideration than was the case in other areas.

Whilst the male Cliffords were interesting, the family is best remembered today for Lady Anne who was less than 5 feet tall, but whose exploits reverberated around the Northern Shires and who was prepared to fight for her rights against either Commonwealth or King although she much preferred the latter. She was born at Skipton Castle, but in the days when women had few legal rights she did not inherit the estate until the last male had died without issue. This was in 1643, by which time she had also been left vast estates on the death of her much older husband, the Earl of Pembroke. In 1643 the Civil War was in full swing and from the 1650s she ignored all opposition and restored her castles including Appleby in Cumbria, Barden Tower in Wharfedale and obviously at Skipton. Over the gatehouse the family motto *Desormais* meaning 'Henceforth' still stands out clearly and defiantly. The lady certainly changed things both at the castle and in the nearby parish church.

There was a church at Skipton long before the Norman Conquest, but the stone structure now known as Holy Trinity dates from the twelfth century. Actually the castle had its own chapel the ruins of which still stand in the grounds. The castle is open on most days of the year on payment of a modest fee. The church is also usually open, and on a wall there is a list of vicars beginning in 1267 just before the living was given to the Canons of Bolton Priory. Following the dissolution in the late 1530s, the living was given to the Dean and Chapter of Christ

Jays breed in many parts of Airedale.

Church, Oxford who hold it to this day. Lady Anne died in 1676 and her will provided for a restoration of the church, but she had also been kind to the building during her lifetime. From 1540 the family burial place was moved from Bolton Priory to All Saints and Lady Anne was careful to ensure that this was in keeping with their status. In 1655 she paid to have 'the steeple of Skipton church built up again because it had been damaged by random cannon balls during the late war.'

We like Skipton because there is so much history and yet there is also plenty of natural history, plus the chance to enjoy a gentle trip on the canal and also on a developing steam railway. On one memorable day the autumn sun still had sufficient strength to make sitting under an old oak tree very pleasant. A treecreeper was working its way up the trunk of another oak and was seeking out insects under some loose strips of bark. Its slim curved bill was full of food, which it suddenly swallowed whilst leaning backwards resting on its tail feathers which are specially strengthened to function as a prop. A gentle breeze rustled the branches and sent the dry brown leaves spinning down towards the woodland floor. A colourful jay picked up fallen acorns from among the leaves and several blackbirds hunted for insects among the litter. All these natural riches we had reached by following the Springs Branch of the canal to its end and we were able to look up at the old quarry and also the castle and the church. Skipton has often been described as the Gateway to the Dales, and although it can be busy, it has retained an air of tranquility.

All it lacks to bring back a complete memory of a bygone age is an old station full of steam trains. Skipton has a rail link and has almost, but not quite, met this requirement, and all one has to do is to follow the signs out of town to Embsay, a distance of just over one mile.

On the board outside the station the Embsay Steam Railway advertises itself as the 'Friendly Line' . . . and it is just that. All the staff of this efficiently run little railway are unpaid volunteers and all the profits are being used to extend the line to the old disused station at Bolton Abbey by the mid-1990s. The more passengers who use this line, the sooner this will be realised.

The line was completed in 1888 to connect Skipton with Bolton Abbey and onwards to Ilkley. The Midland Railway was obliged to keep the line in good condition because this was a Royal Route, with monarchs and princes visiting the Duke of Devonshire to shoot grouse on the land around Bolton Abbey. In its heyday the line was also busy carrying tourists to Bolton Abbey and then on to Ilkley which in the 1890s was an important spa town. How sad it is to see the present state of the once-proud Bolton Abbey station which has deteriorated rapidly since the line closed to passenger traffic as a result of the Beeching cuts. The line carried stone until 1968 and was then derelict until in 1979 the society began by operating a service between Emsay and Holywell Halt.

The wooden ticket office used by the society once stood outside Ilkley station where it was used as a shelter by the drivers of horse-drawn cabs. The former station office and waiting room have been converted into a shop concentrating upon railway and travel books as well as those dealing with mining. Model railway enthusiasts are also able to buy rolling stock.

The ladies' waiting room is now the cafe and what was the

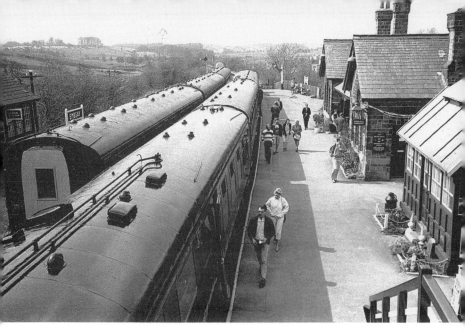

The station at Embsay provides a reminder of the Victorian Age of steam.

porters' lamp room is the kitchen. There are excellent views of the station from the recently restored footbridge leading to platform 2. The waiting room here now houses a display of photographs showing the line during its heyday. Across the large free car park is the goods yard weighbridge, now converted by the Northern Mining Research Group into a small museum of lead mining. On Open Days and on most Bank Holidays this area is full of noise and colour as barrel and steam organs belch out vibrant music and Morris dancers add their own unique contribution.

Following the closure of the line it was intended to preserve the branch line to Grassington which strikes off just before Embsay, and the Embsay to Grassington Railway Preservation Society was founded in 1968. The construction of a bypass road and the needs of the Tilcon quarry meant those plans had to be altered, and the society therefore looked the other way from Embsay towards Holywell Halt, where a picnic site has been carefully landscaped. Yet another feature of this line is the accessibility of country walks, and leaflets listing these can be purchased from the shop.

The run-up to Holywell Halt is slow and leisurely and there are several stops which allow you to use the train as a bird hide.

Regular 'supper excursions' are organised and passengers can enjoy seeing wildlife by moonlight; the gas-lit station at Embsay brings back real memories of rail travel at the turn of the century.

We look forward to the day when the link to Bolton Abbey in Wharfedale is complete – Skipton will then have another reason to call itself 'The Gateway to the Dales'.

A Santa Special on the Embsay line.

The pied flycatcher breeds in the woodlands around Skipton.

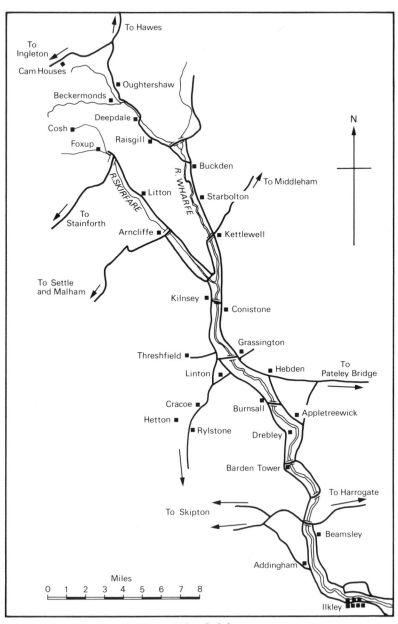

Wharfedale.

CHAPTER 5

Wharfedale

Rising in the hills towards the Craven Highlands, the Wharfe flows eastwards for around 60 miles before merging with the muddy waters of the Ouse and then on to the Humber. It is a dale of magnificent scenery with the valley sides in the upper reaches composed of cliffs of exposed limestone surmounted by Yoredale rocks, and reef knolls – areas of thick limestone which once formed part of the seabed – also add interest to the landscape. It has history and natural history in abundance, its only disadvantage being that it is an easy dale to drive and is situated close to the towns and cities of Lancashire and especially West Yorkshire. This means that Wharfedale is one of the busiest of the Dales and yet each village has its own dignified method of absorbing the mass of tourists.

The Wharfe is a swift clear clean river formed by the merging of two mountain streams at Beckermonds which means 'the mouth of the becks'. The name implies Norse influence in this area, as elsewhere in the Dales. Those with the energy to seek the source must follow the main feeder stream high onto Cam Fell close to the line of the Old Roman road between Ingleton in the Craven Dales and Bainbridge in Wensleydale. Cam means 'a ridge of hills'. Beckermonds itself is around 1000 feet (305 metres) above sea level, and by the time the infant Wharfe has reached Hubberholme at 800 feet (244 metres) it has passed through Langstrothdale, which in effect is Upper Wharfedale. Although the river is fairly narrow here, it makes a considerable amount of happy noise as it tumbles over flat slabs of limestone on which grow cushions of English stonecrop and sky-blue flowers of harebell. The lime-rich water supports a flourishing invertebrate life which is fed upon by resident dippers and grey wagtails. In the summer this is also wheatear and common sandpiper country. The small hamlets of Langstrothdale have their own secrets including the Bronze Age circle of twenty stones above Yockenthwaite set on the north side of the river. The name 'thwaite' again proves

Norse origins for this now tiny hamlet, but there are records to show that it was once much larger with its own inn and school. There is an ancient green road over the Horse Head Pass to Foxup in Littondale. Deepdale also has its share of ancient history in the form of an Iron Age village on the west side of a hill about 1600 feet (487 metres) above sea level, whilst in the modern village there is a graceful little bridge close to some old farmhouses.

It is well worth the effort to visit Oughtershaw Beck and its confluence with Greenfield Beck near Beckermonds because this is regarded as the true source of the Wharfe in what was the hunting forest of Langstrothdale. From Greenfields itself there is an ancient packhorse track skirting round Birkwill Moor and on to Horton-in-Ribblesdale. This was the ancient trade route into Lancashire. From Oughtershaw which is 1200 feet (365 metres) up there is another track over Fleet Moss to Hawes. These isolated little settlements are often missed by casual tourists who do not venture beyond Hubberholme and think that the Wharfe begins just beyond the sturdy little church.

Hubberholme was named after a Viking chieftain and is famed for its church of St Michael and All Angels and the George Inn which was once the vicarage. The church is older than either Fountains Abbey or Bolton Abbey and the massive squat tower is thirteenth century but its main claim to fame is the rood loft dating from 1558, and one of the very few left in England. Its original function was to hold the rood or crucifix, and at the Reformation most were ripped out in an effort to stamp out 'popery'. The choir stalls and the pews are modern and were fashioned by Thompson of Kilburn whose trade mark is a mouse carved in some hidden corner. It provides tourists with a great deal of fun trying to pit their wits against a master craftsman by finding his mouse. There is also a memorial to the author J.B. Priestley (1894-1984) who was born in Bradford and loved the Dales in general and Hubberholme in particular.

Across the bridge from the church is the George Inn which still has some connection with the old way of life when on New Year's Day the Hubberholme 'Parliament' meets. Local farmers bid for the tenancy of Kirkgill pasture, a 16-acre field, and the

Hubberholme Church.

money raised now goes towards a 'do' for the local old age pensioners, but in the days when it was needed it went to support the poor of the parish.

This is walking country and our favourite stroll winds around the church and alongside the river. Here on one glorious day in early June we watched a female goosander with her eleven chicks all bobbing about on a swift current and trying gamely to fish. Close by is the hamlet of Cray, where there is a splendid tumble of waterfalls, and at the White Lion Inn are displayed the antlers of the last red deer to be killed in the valley.

The centre of deer hunting was the next settlement downdale, the aptly named Buckden, which straddles a once-vital crossroads. The inn is appropriately named The Buck. There is a route into Hawes via Fleet Moss and another via Cray and Kidstones Pass into Bishopdale and thence to Aysgarth in Wensleydale. The village lies snugly beneath the bulk of Buckden Pike which at 2302 feet (701 metres) easily qualifies as a mountain and presents a challenge even to the serious walker. There is a good car park and an attractive picnic site. Another route up to the Pike starts from Starbotton and follows yet another green road up the Knuckle Bone to the

The Rood Loft, Hubberholme.

summit. The grey limestone village had to be rebuilt during the latter half of the seventeenth century because it was far too close to the river and was almost completely swept away during the great flood of 1686 which claimed many lives. The neat cottages clustered around the Fox and Hounds, however, are a great attraction and can be used as a centre for walks into the

Kilnsey Crag and trout farm.

small dales of Coverdale and Waldendale as well as over to Arncliffe.

Kettlewell was very important between the twelfth and sixteenth centuries when the monks were the effective rulers of much of England. Cradled firmly by the Pennine fells, dark grey cottages, inns and church all lie along Cam Beck which tumbles down from Great Whernside. This is walker and tourist country, now so serene that it is difficult to imagine that this was a centre for lead mining, and no doubt the Bluebell built in 1680, the Racehorses and King's Head inns saw many a rough night. These days they serve to slake the thirst of hardy walkers on the Dales Way, a long-distance footpath linking Ilkley with Windermere, four miles of which lie between Kettlewell and Buckden. The church, built between 1882 and 1885, is rather a pleasant building considering the unimaginative times during which it was built. There is a carved font inside, which came from the Norman church which once stood on the site. Standing in the village, you will find the mountain scenery which surrounds Kettlewell strangely

71

Some of the finest Dale scenery is seen around Halton Gill.

inspiring. Great Whernside dominates the eastern aspect with Top Mere to the north and Knipe Scar to the west. Travelling downdale for three miles leads to Kilnsey Crag, one of Britain's most dramatic rock formations favoured by climbers – and peregrines too.

Just beyond the Crag is Kilnsey Park, open on most days on payment of a small fee and fast becoming one of Wharfedale's most popular tourist attractions. A pony-trekking centre caters for both beginners and experienced riders who can enjoy first-hand some of the green roads which are a feature of this area. There is also a freshwater Aquarium and River Life Centre plus informative videos depicting life around and within the Wharfe. It is possible to buy rainbow trout bred in the ponds which can be fed with food bought from the shop. Day fishing tickets are also for sale and the car park and picnic site are extensive and provide excellent views of the Crag. The village itself developed around a grange of Fountains Abbey which was on the green road of Mastiles which crosses the fells here. It is still possible to follow Mastiles Lane on foot from Kilnsey where a fragment of the Abbey grange still stands.

At the height of a busy tourist season in Wharfedale, where can peace be found? We would say in Littondale which is one of the most underrated of the minor dales. It is reached from

The Falcon Inn at Arncliffe – still half hotel, half farm, which is a perfect combination.

Kilnsey by following the River Skirfare from the point where it joins the Wharfe to its source on the hills beyond Foxup and Halton towards the slopes of Penyghent. The Dale takes its name from the charming village of Litton but the most attractive of the settlements is at Arncliffe. The lovely old church of St Oswald overlooks the Skirfare and is seen at its best when viewed from the bridge even though it is screened by trees. The tower is fifteenth century with the rest being eighteenth century, although there has been a church on the site from Saxon times. The village, built of limestone, is set around a huge green on which stands an old pump and the Falcon Inn which is still part-pub and part-farm. Arncliffe is yet another ideal centre for walkers with a riverside footpath signposted from the bridge to Kettlewell. There are also walks leading upstream where beds of flat limestone are exposed along the river which, considering it is only a tributary of the Wharfe, is surprisingly substantial. It is said that the name Arncliffe means the cliff on which the eagle nests, the Old English name for an eagle being the Erne.

The next settlement down the Wharfe itself is Grassington, the main tourist centre in the Dale, and offering a great variety

Morris dancers performing in Grassington Square.

of accommodation for visitors. Just the mention of Grassington brings back to us a flood of memories: the Morris dancers in the square on a hot Sunday over Easter; a May Sunday spent dodging the showers in Grass Woods; a June scorcher among the flowers of the limestone meadows above the old lead mines; a cool wet September morning fishing the Wharfe for trout; and whilst writing this chapter a day with sleet in the air mingling with the crowds in the square.

It is fitting that there should be a Yorkshire Dales National Park Centre on the outskirts of the village, and there is an extensive and reasonably priced car park here. Archaeologists have shown that settlers were present in the Grassington area during the Bronze Age, there was an Iron-Age village just to the north of the present one, and close to the entrance of Grass Woods is the so-called Fort Gregory. This was a Brigantes settlement and the tribe offered stiff resistance to the Romans. Imperial might eventually succeeded and there is a Roman road running across the higher part of the village which probably connected with the substantial fort at Bainbridge in Wensleydale, and also with another fort at Olicana which we know today as Ilkley.

After the Romans left, the next settlers to control the area were the Angles who built a village around a little stream which

Linton – the Parish Church of Grassington.

is now confined to a Styx-like existence, being culverted beneath the square. When the Normans settled the area they named it Ghersinstone and a market charter was granted in 1281, but it may have been too close to Skipton to develop into an important trading centre. Visitors to Grassington do not realise that it is not the product of medieval agriculture but of the intensive eighteenth- and nineteenth-century lead-mining industry. At this time it would have been a rough place with the hard-working, hard-drinking miners letting off steam in the alehouses. The old mine workings are reached via Moor Road from the top of Main Street and then on to Yarnbury where the mine manager's house is situated. Over the moorland is a mass of spoil heaps dominated by a tall smelt mill chimney with a long arched grass-covered flue leading towards it. Nature is healing the wounds of industry but only slowly. This process can be appreciated by walking over Grassington Moor to Conistone which reveals the scars of industry among impressive clints and grykes (see page 13) plus meadows rich in flowers including rock rose, Yorkshire milkwort, meadow saxifrage and bird's eye primrose.

Linton Falls, which once provided water to drive the mill.

To discover more about Grassington as a working village a visit should be made to the Upper Wharfedale Museum, housed in two converted lead miners' cottages overlooking the square. This wonderful jumble is run by volunteers and is usually open on payment of a nominal fee at weekends and on most days during the tourist season. On chilly days a welcoming fire blazes in the hearth and coffee and tea are served in the tiny kitchen. The display of Wharfedale farming, mining and domestic life is informative and the village itself is a joy to the historian. The Old Hall tucked away behind the Devonshire Hotel is said to be the oldest inhabited house in the dale, some parts being thirteenth-century, although there have obviously been additions and alterations since then. A considerable amount of medieval ornamental stonework and some Tudor mullioned windows combine to ensure that the hall is a Grade 1 listed building.

Church House is close to the square and has often been mistaken for the Old Hall. It bears the date and the initials SAP. This was once the residence of one Stephen Peart and his wife Anne. There was a time when the house and its attached stables were a focal point for travellers, a fact first realised by

Burnsall 'Grammar School', still in use by younger children.

the Airey family who were carriers and then by Kit Chapman who ran a mail-coach business between Skipton and Buckden. This was still thriving around 1900, the departure of the coaches being controlled by a clock, almost certainly the one which now overlooks the square. It is only recently that Stephen Peart's old dwelling has been known as Church House. Visitors soon notice that there is no parish church in Grassington, and worshippers have to follow the Wharfe downstream to Linton, not an easy thing to do on a cold winter's night for those without transport. Parish functions are now held in Peart's house, hence the change of name to Church House.

Grassington once had its own rail link with the station situated at nearby Threshfield. In its heyday Bradford businessmen lived in Grassington and travelled to the wool markets on 'The Residential Express'. It was certainly the railway which allowed the old lead-mining centre to become a tourist attraction. It was planned to push the Yorkshire Dales Railway right up to Kettlewell and to link it via a 3½-mile tunnel to the main York to Darlington line. The project never got beyond linking Embsay to Grassington (see Chapter 4). The line opened in 1902 and closed to all traffic in 1969. The track still runs to the limeworks at Swinden but the track to Grassington has long since been lifted. What a boon it would have been if a steam railway could have run from Skipton into Wharfedale, but alas the opportunity has gone for ever.

The cottages at Chamber End Fold are seventeenth-century miners' cottages, and although restored at some expense they still retain their character. The terms 'chamber' and 'fold' are both worthy of explanation. The word 'chamber' indicates that at one time one of the houses functioned as a court house dealing with minor and local offences. The word 'fold' means a narrow alleyway leading into a courtyard. The so-called Town Hall, also known as the Devonshire Institute, was once the Mechanics' Institute. It was built in 1855 with money provided by the Duke of Devonshire.

To reach the parish church one of two routes can be followed to Linton – down along a narrow footpath from the Information Centre and over a small bridge, but we prefer to follow the main road to Grassington Bridge and then turn along a field path to the church. In 1603 a stone bridge was built to replace a wooden structure and in the eighteenth century it was strengthened and widened and the steep approaches were eased. The original shape can be seen beneath the more modern masonry.

Linton is a tiny unspoiled village with an old packhorse bridge, a fine inn and its very own Dick Whittington. We often enjoy a summer picnic in the middle of Linton Green or take a winter lunch at the Fountaine Inn. Richard Fountaine left the dales to make his fortune in London but never forgot his home, and when he died in 1721 he left money to construct almshouses for six folk at Linton. The 'hospital' was designed by Sir John Vanbrugh who constructed for each inhabitant a self-contained cottage linked to a lovely chapel. It is still maintained by the rents obtained from land around Grassington, Threshfield and Hebden. The packhorse bridge is mentioned in the fourteenth century; it was repaired by Dame Elizabeth Redmayne in the mid-eighteenth century and still carries her name.

Some distance from the green is the ancient church of St Michael and All Angles which dominates the banks of the Wharfe. It serves Threshfield, Linton and Grassington and is

The Bridge at Burnsall.

thought to have been established long before the Norman
Conquest, at a time when the Danes were settled in the area.
The historian Allcrof pointed out that churches dedicated to St
Michael tend to be sited in remote areas. This was in order to
pay homage to a man who supported the Jewish people in their
fight against the pagans and who had to build their places of
worship away from the main settlements. Thus when remote
areas were chosen, St Michael was likely to be chosen as the
saint. Churches established early in Danish-controlled Britain
were likely to be remotely sited, also away from the pagans.
The present building was begun around 1150 but among its
many interesting artefacts is a brass crucifix which is thought to
be Romanesque and dates from around the ninth or tenth
century. Close by the stile-like entrance to the church are two
cottages known as 'kirk yett' which were once an inn. This takes
us back to the days when many of the congregation travelled so
far to worship that provision had to be made for an overnight
stay when the weather was bad. A footpath from Linton church
follows a riverside footpath to Burnsall.

As the river winds its way through limestone gorges towards
Burnsall there is a splendid view up to the right to the twelfth-
century parish church of St Wilfrid and the Elizabethan
grammar school. Inside the church are the remnants of what

would seem to have been a number of Anglian crosses, and there is a good example of a Norse-Danish font. There are also fragments of tenth-century hogback gravestones. Here too are the village stocks with the exit onto the steep road guarded by an unusual lychgate operated by an ingenious system of weights. The school and attached master's house is a most interesting building founded in 1605 by William Craven of Appletreewick, little altered since and still in use as the village school. The upper storey was divided into dormitory chambers by solid oak planks, and these can still be seen today. Beyond the graceful bridge is a spacious village green overlooking the river and dominated by a tall maypole, and there are plenty of seats for those who want to picnic. There is a pay car park beyond the green, but at peak times this soon fills up, as do the tea shops and the tables of the Red Lion Hotel which serves bar snacks. Each August the green is the site of the Burnsall Sports, which have taken place since the sixteenth century, the main event being the race to the top of Burnsall Fell and back.

Between Linton and Burnsall is the village of Thorpe-in-the-Hollow which, because of its secluded position, escaped the attentions of the marauding Scots in the early fourteenth century. Local folk new its value and moved to Thorpe in times of danger. It is said that the principal occupation hereabouts was cobbling, the menfolk making and mending the footwear of the monks from Fountains Abbey.

Appletreewick was once owned by the monks of Bolton Priory and we wonder if it was once an orchard, but from the Middle Ages it was famous for its onion fair. There are two old inns and a number of cottages once belonging to merchants and yeomen, whilst just beyond the village is Parcevall Hall, a restored seventeenth-century building now used as an Anglican diocesan house. It is surrounded by sixteen acres of terraced gardens and woodlands which are open daily from Easter to 31st October between 10 a.m. and 6 p.m. There is a picnic area from which there are magnificent views, and refreshments are available. The village has three old halls. Monks Hall was a grange belonging to Bolton Abbey; High Hall was built in 1549 for the Craven family; and Low Hall is of unknown age but was restored by William Preston in 1658. It is said that the latter

The Clifford Almshouses,

Beamsley, Wharfedale.

once had a particularly noisy and stubborn ghost which was excorcised only with difficulty.

Just downstream of Appletreewick is Barden Bridge, and above this is the ruin of a fifteenth-century tower which was once a hunting lodge belonging to the Clifford family. There is a car park and a restaurant here but there is no fee to visit the building, into which is set a stone carving recording the fact that it was restored by Lady Anne Clifford.

From Barden Bridge a long footpath winds through the Strid Woods to Bolton Priory which has a very large riverside parking area for which a fee is required. There is also a substantial cafe and a bookshop. There is also an entry fee to the Strid Woods Nature Trails which run through deciduous woodlands. At Burnsall, the Wharfe is a wide river and at Bolton Priory it is just as substantial. Between the two, however, the rushing water is squeezed between towering rocks and the area is known as the Strid. It may derive the name because it looks to be 'stridable' but it is far too wide and dangerous for this to be attempted.

We may have caused some confusion by referring to both Bolton Abbey and Bolton Priory. Abbeys were inhabited by monks who were rather insular and their religious services were private affairs. The Priory brethren, on the other hand, were more outgoing and mixed much more with the local folk who were allowed to attend Mass. At the Dissolution the Priory churches were saved because they were used by the local people and could become their parish church. Bolton Priory was established in 1154 on land overlooking the Wharfe given by Alice de Romilly whose mother had given the Augustinians lands at Embsay in Airedale in 1120. The land there proved unsuitable and the brethren removed to Bolton. By 1220 the church, chapter house and domestic buildings had probably been completed. Compared to Yorkshire's Fountains, Bolton was never a rich establishment but there were 200 people here including monks and lay brethren. There were a number of outlying granges which controlled the sheep pastures and lead mines. Like the rest of the area the Priory suffered from the Scots raids during the early fourteenth century, and it is said that the brethren eventually employed a number of 'armed gentlemen' to make up what was in effect a private army.

The Manor House Museum at Ilkley.

The Priory is open daily free of charge; there is a sales point for books and very often there are guides available. After the Dissolution the area gradually came under the control of the Duke of Devonshire who built a fine shooting lodge onto the old gatehouse. Spanning the road is a very narrow archway which taxes the skill and nerves of coach drivers and which once carried an aqueduct feeding the abbey mill. There is another car park and information centre in the village. There is a fine walk down to the Priory from the car park which crosses a wooden bridge overlooking a solid set of stepping stones over the Wharfe. To the left of the descent to the bridge there are a number of depressions in the lush fields which mark the position of the old monastic fish ponds. These rich pastures once fed the famous Craven Heifer bred here by the Rev. W. Carr, who also laid out the paths through Strid Woods. This beast weighed in at 312 stones 8lbs (1956 kg) and is celebrated in the name of many local hostelries. It is probable that the first to be so named was the inn between Skipton and Grassington on the right of the road. It is still possible to see that the building was once a farm with an alehouse attached.

From Bolton Priory the Wharfe meanders its way towards Bolton Bridge close to the Devonshire Arms, and it is at this point that the National Park officially ends. We have always considered that Wharfedale begins and ends at Ilkley, and so we continue beyond Bolton Bridge and explore Beamsley, Addingham and Ilkley, Beamsley, overlooked by Beacon Hill, is difficult to explore these days because it is split by the main Skipton to Harrogate road but the ancient route wound its way through the settlement. Just to the left of the modern road is an archway bearing the coat of arms of the Clifford family. Through this is a circular complex of almshouses dated 1593 and founded by the mother of Lady Anne Clifford. Here live seven old ladies, each in a self-contained dwelling set around a chapel. In our view this is the finest building in Wharfedale.

Addingham is an industrial village once devoted to domestic, as opposed to factory, weaving. The uppermost of the three storeys in the cottages was the weaving area, its elevation ensuring that the maximum use was made of the available light. Once a crossroads on the old turnpike system, it is but a short trot from the relatively new settlement of Addingham to the ancient market town of Ilkley, an ideal base from which to explore Wharfedale.

Everyone knows the tune of 'ILKLA MOOR BART AT', said to have been composed by members of a Halifax church choir whilst they were enjoying a picnic around the Cow and Calf rocks high up above the town which is known as the Heather Spa. This affectionate name recalls Ilkley's years of glory when its health-giving springs and bracing moorland walks established it as a place to come to seek the cure. White Wells is an eighteenth-century bath house which has been restored and is open to the public at weekends and on Bank Holidays. The railway age of the mid-nineteenth century turned Ilkley, like Grassington, into a retreat for wealthy Bradford wool merchants. The Elizabethan Manor House Museum, which is open daily except Mondays, traces the history of Ilkley from the time when it was an important Roman fort called Olicana guarding the crossing of the Wharfe. High on the hills overlooking the town is the famous Swastika stone, the only one in Britain and a prehistoric carving of an ancient symbol for fire, and there are also examples of 'cup and ring' stones, found in the town itself. Here too are impressive Christian relics within the parish church of All Saints. The Ilkley crosses are fragments which have been jigsawed together. Others can

The Ilkley Crosses – once brightly coloured and displayed outside, thus pre-dating the first church.

be seen in the Manor House Museum. Their sheer quantity suggests the presence of an Anglo-Saxon cemetery and the crosses may have been grave markers. Some scholars have suggested that there may have been a pre-Viking monastery on the site. When the crosses are seen in the recesses of the church or on a pedestal in a museum they look grey and scholarly, but when newly erected they would have been brightly painted and standing proudly in meadows of flowers high above the meandering Wharfe. They must have been an impressive Christian focus.

Before leaving Ilkley, we can never resist a final visit to the Wharfe where it lives up to its name of the 'swift' river and pulses beneath the ancient bridge. There is plenty of parking on the riverside and walks lead along the banks and up into extensive woodlands. Boats are for hire during the summer and there are plenty of cafes, hotels, toilets and a fine playground for children.

Now restricted to pedestrians, Ilkley old bridge has three spans of very graceful proportions and must have been a vital crossing point in the days of the packhorse. Such bridges tended to be narrow and have low parapets so that the baskets carried by the horses could hang over the edge and not bump into the walls and cause damange to any delicate loads.

From Ilkley the Wharfe runs through Otley, birthplace in 1718 of Thomas Chippendale the furniture maker, and then across the Vale of York to its junction with the Ouse at Cawood.

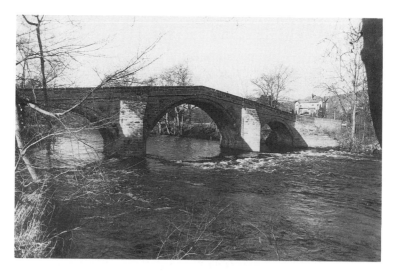

Ilkley Bridge.

The birthplace of Thomas Chippendale in Otley, with a plaque on the wall (see below).

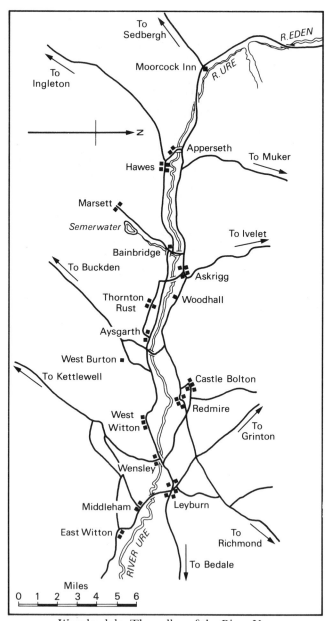

To Sedbergh

R. EDEN

R. URE

Moorcock Inn

To Ingleton

N

Apperseth

Hawes

To Muker

Marsett

Semerwater

To Ivelet

Bainbridge

Askrigg

To Buckden

Thornton Rust

Woodhall

Aysgarth

West Burton

Castle Bolton

To Kettlewell

Redmire

West Witton

To Grinton

Wensley

Middleham

Leyburn

East Witton

RIVER URE

To Richmond

To Bedale

Miles

0 1 2 3 4 5 6

Wensleydale. The valley of the River Ure.

CHAPTER 6

The Ure and Wensleydale

From its source on Lands Fell above Hawes the Ure flows sixty miles before its substantial waters are absorbed by the tiny trickle of the Ouse, which for some reason gives its name to the union. The Ure flows through some of the most majestic scenery in Britain. Here we are concerned with the Yorkshire Dales and only follow the course in detail as far as Ripon, an ideal centre for the tourist.

Within a few miles of its source the Ure picks up water from Cotterdale, Mossdale, Fossdale and Widdale, and as it reaches Appersett the river is already substantial. Cotter Force is a dramatic waterfall and the haunt of dipper and grey wagtail, whilst on the surrounding hillsides the piping call of the golden plover is a feature of springtime. Appersett derives from the Norse *saetre* and means a summer pasture. A graceful old bridge spans Widdale Beck close to its junction with the Ure and the broad green is sufficiently unaltered to enable the pattern of the medieval village to be seen. On the opposite bank at Hardrow is one of Britain's most famous waterfalls which certainly has the most unusual approach. Admission is through the Green Dragon Inn on payment of a modest fee. At around 100 feet (30.5 metres), the falls are claimed to be the highest in England and it is said that Blondin crossed the gap over the gorge on a tightrope, pausing halfway across to cook an omelette! The falls are set in a natural amphitheatre in which a podium was built and brass band concerts held from around 1885. These were revived in 1990 and deserve to be supported. What better spot to listen to the music of Black Dyke Mills, Hammonds Sauce Works and Bess O' th' Barn mingling with the sound of falling water and soaring skylark?

Just as the Aire rises in Malhamdale and is never allowed to include its name in that of the valley, so the Ure is Wensleydale's river. Many feel that we should call the river the Wensley or revert to the old name of Uredale or the even more ancient Yoredale. Until the eighteenth century Upper

D

Wensleydale was very remote. Before the turnpike road was driven through in the 1760s only the Roman road through Bainbridge offered anything resembling an easy passage. Even Hawes, now regarded as the capital of Upper Wensleydale, was isolated and Askrigg was the market centre. Hawes did not have a charter until 1699. Except on Tuesday which is market day, parking is usually possible along the main street, but there is a large car park close to the old railway station. This has now been converted into an Information Centre with the engine sheds of 1883 housing a Museum of Dales Life which is open daily on payment of a small fee. Hawes station was once an important junction linking Wensleydale with the Settle to Carlisle line via Garsdale. Nearby is Outhwaite's rope works, now with an associated gift shop, and watching the traditional method of platting rope, even on such a modest scale, is just one of the treats which Hawes has to offer. Close by is a Quaker burial ground which was given to the Friends by Oswald Routh in 1680.

The view over the town and valley from St Margaret's church is spectacular but the church itself only dates to 1851. From the church a flagged causeway called Bealey Bank winds its way to Gayle village.

From the beckside at Gayle, narrow winding entries lead to stone cottages. Traffic still has to pass over a ford, and just over the retaining wall is a set of steps once used by women who did their washing in the beck. Looking downstream from the packhorse bridge, the eye is drawn towards a now disused cotton mill but the wooden leet to the waterwheel is still intact although the wheel itself has gone. A circular stroll can be completed by returning to Hawes along Gayle Lane on which is the creamery where the famous Wensleydale cheese is made. We feel that it is a pity that the building is not often open to the public, with perhaps a small museum devoted to the history of cheesemaking. It can, however, be visited by prior arrangement. An earlier creamery, now closed, is situated near Hawes Bridge looking upstream along Gayle Beck, with the fading words still visible on the cumbling walls.

The banks of the Ure are straddled by a chain of delightful villages, none more magnetic than Bainbridge, sandwiched betweeen the meandering river and Semerwater. This is a

Hawes village and church.

haunting lake and an unusual feature in a county which has only two natural lakes – Malham Tarn and Semerwater. Bainbridge is dominated by a steep grassy mound, now part of a private farm but once the site of Virosidium, a Roman fort staffed by 500 legionaries. Above the modern road to Hawes runs the Roman highway called Cam Road which linked Bainbridge and Ribchester on the Ribble. Below the fort is Low Mill which is open to visitors each summer Wednesday and Friday from 2pm to 5pm. The blowing of the Bainbridge Horn takes place occasionally between Holy Rood (27th September) and Shrove Tuesday when a member of the Metcalfe family blasts out the far-carrying sound at 9pm. Some have suggested that this dates back to Roman times and served to guide soldiers returning through the then thick forest to the fort on the hill. When not in action the horn is kept in the entrance of the Rose and Crown Hotel. This was established in 1445 and was partly rebuilt in Georgian times. It overlooks the large green on which stand the stocks. An apron in front of

Pinfold Cottage next to the Post Office marks the place where shepherds brought stray sheep to await collection by their rightful owners. There is also an interesting chapel and a building which was once the Dames School.

Bainbridge has two graceful bridges, the one over the Ure designed by John Carr of York. The other crosses the Bain, a tributary of the Ure which flows out of Semerwater around one mile away, and is said to be England's shortest named river.

Semerewater is a naturalist's paradise of around 25 hectares (62.5 acres) and is an S.S.S.I. (Site of Special Scientific Interest). The lake is glacial in origin, its water being held back by debris known as moraine. In winter it is a haven for wildfowl including pochard, tufted duck and the noisy but always alert whooper swans. In summer when the birds have returned north to their breeding grounds Semerwater is used by wind surfers.

It is probable that a tribe of ancient Britons who caused the Romans such problems had their dwellings supported on stilts over the lake. The local legend of the 'drowned city of Semerwater' may therefore have some basis in fact. The erratics left by the melting glacier are strewn along the shore, where there is ample parking space. One large boulder called the Carlow Stone is said to have had some religious significance for these ancient people.

On the opposite bank of the Ure is the substantial village of Askrigg, made famous as the location for the TV series 'All Creatures Great and Small'. Askrigg, which means 'the ridge on which the ash trees grow', was mentioned in the Domesday Book but did not receive a market charter until 1587. Close to the fifteenth-century church, which has some splendid beaming in the nave, is a bull ring set in the cobbles, a relic of the barbarous days when it was believed that baiting the poor beast tenderised its flesh.

When the Richmond to Lancaster turnpike was routed through Askrigg its future was assured because the local industries of clock making, hand knitting, lead mining and textile manufacture had new markets opened up to them. There is a route from Askrigg over the fells into Swaledale, but our trip down Wensleydale takes us to Aysgarth via Nappa Hall and Caperby. Although Nappa Hall is not open to the public,

A junior member of the Metcalfe family blowing the Bainbridge Horn.

its grounds are criss-crossed by footpaths. It is a fortified manor house built in the mid-fifteenth-century by Thomas Metcalfe who, with his Wensleydale archers, played a significant part in the Battle of Agincourt in 1415. Caperby is yet another of Wensleydale's ancient markets, and a cross surmounting a set of high steps was erected in 1674 but the actual charter dates from 1305. The village had strong Quaker connections and George Fox himself preached here. The Friends' Meeting house, although built in 1864, was constructed on classical lines.

We once passed through Caperby early on a winter's morning and the sun was casting shadows over the frosted fields, enabling us to notice the old cultivation terraces which were used to grow crops, particularly corn. They are called lynchets and are typical of medieval farming practices. We were en route to Bolton Castle, one of Yorkshire's most spectacular ruins. Built by the first Lord Scrope in 1397, Bolton Castle was well fortified but great store was placed on comfort. It is said to have taken eighteen years to build and cost £12,000, an enormous sum in those days. Mary Queen of Scots was imprisoned here between July 1658 and January 1659, a fact which has led to its recent restoration as one of Wensleydale's tourist attractions. It is open daily between March and mid-November from 10am to 5pm. The village which nestles below the castle is a delight, especially the tiny Norman church of St Oswald's which houses a small museum displaying aspects of Wensleydale's history and natural history. On the outer wall of the church is a weathered example of a mass dial, the forerunner of the sundial. Marks were scraped into the stone and in the centre was a hole into which was poked a stick. Mass was held when the shadow fell on the appropriate radiating scratch. At present it is difficult to see how it worked because so little light now strikes the wall due to the shadow cast by the castle. We should remember, however, that the church is more than 200 years older than the castle.

Another very similar Norman church dedicated to St Mary is within walking distance of Bolton Castle. St Mary's Redmire is now administered with St Oswald's as one parish as the population has declined following the closure of the local lead mines. The scars of these are still evident around Bolton, Redmire and Preston-under-Scar. Lead mining here was never as profitable as in Swaledale and Wharfedale but stone quarries, plus butter and cheese production, ensured and still ensure a healthy economy. Close to Redmire's old market cross is an ancient oak and a quoits pitch. This game is played on a pitch with what is called a hob at either end, separated by a distance of eleven yards. The hob is a short metal rod about five inches high and set into the ground. The idea is to stand over one hob, run two paces and hurl a steel quoit, which weighs five pounds, at the other hob. If the hob is circled it is called a 'ringer' and counts two points. The opposition can counter this by covering an opponent's quoit with their own, in which case it has been successfully 'topped'. Teams of between nine and eleven players compete fiercely in leagues which run from mid-May to September.

West Burton and Aysgarth are situated on the opposite bank of the Ure, the former never having had either a market or a church. It was, however, a vital settlement as it controlled the track over to Buckden and into Wharfedale. Its long

West Burton Green.

rectangular green is dominated by an obelisk surmounting a set of steps erected in 1820. West Burton was a mining village but its origins are pre-Conquest and it still has an unspoilt beauty, especially around Burton Force, a lovely waterfall which once powered the village mill.

But Yorkshire's most famous falls are at Aysgarth where there is a substantial visitor centre and a car park close to the three falls which are linked by footpaths through lovely stretches of woodland. As Dorothy Wordsowrth noted in 1802, the falls are particularly spectacular after rain or during a period of snow-melt. Some idea of what the Dale was like in the coaching days can be got from visiting Yore Mill, once a cotton mill constructed around 1785 but rebuilt after a fire of 1853 and powered by water from the Upper Falls. This has now been converted into a Carriage Museum with exhibits including coaches, maps of the turnpike roads, post horns, coachmen's uniforms and materials dating to the days of the packhorse. Yore Mill has also a claim to international fame. During the 1860s the mill produced a surplus of red cloth which was sold off cheaply to an Italian and was made into uniforms for Garibaldi's famous red army.

St Andrew's Church, one of the largest in Yorkshire, partly dates from 1268 and has a churchyard occupying 4½ acres.

95

The scale and magnificence of the interior show its importance, and during the fourteenth-century three members of the influential Neville family were Rectors here and Alexander Neville became Archbishop of York in 1374. To celebrate this event an enormous feast was held which lasted for three days and on the menu were curlews, swans, pigs, sheep and oxen. The high price paid for coneys (rabbits) indicates just how rare they were in the fourteenth-century, having been introduced justs after the Norman Conquest for their fur and as a luxury food. Between Aysgarth and Leyburn there is a substantial wall running around the summit of a small hill, topped by a few straggling conifers. This is what remains of an old warren in which rabbits were protected from poachers. The man in charge was called either Coney or Warrener. We wonder what modern farmers would think of this protection as they struggle to grow crops in the presence of ever-hungry rabbits?

Inside Aysgarth church is an exquisite wooden screen which fills the south side of the chancel and which was brought here when Jervaulx Abbey was dissolved around 1540. It was fashioned in 1506 by the Ripon School of Carvers who also did wonderful work in their own Cathedral. Another reminder of Jervaulx is the vicar's stall, made from two bench ends, also brought here at the Dissolution.

The village of Wensley is also dominated by its church overlooking the Ure Bridge. Holy Trinity church has a nave and chancel dating back to the thirteenth-century, although it probably replaced an eighth-century Saxon church. Installed in the church by the third Duke of Bolton is a set of box pews which produce a theatrical effect. He did this because his wife had been an actress and liked theatre boxes with curtains! There is a wooden screen and a reliquary which is thought to be unique in England and to have once held the mortal remains of St. Agatha, brought from Easby Abbey in Swaledale. There is a fine collection of brasses and those who wish to take rubbings can do so by contacting the vicarage and paying a small fee. The best in the collection commemorates Sir Simon de Wenslawe, a fourteenth-century priest.

Wensley was once the most important town in the Dale to which it gave its name, and the market charter is dated 1202. As populations increased and communications improved, rival

Aysgarth Falls.

markets developed, but tradition would have prevailed had it not been for the Black Death, which struck in 1563. The parish records reveal many deaths whilst most of the survivors moved to Leyburn, as did the market traders, who never returned. The present attractive appearance of Wensley, which is an estate village, is due to Charles Powlett who married the daughter of the last Lord Scrope and assumed the title of his father-in-law. The gates to Bolton Hall, which he built in 1678, face the post office across the green, and although almost rebuilt after a fire in 1902, the main shell of the early house remains. Although it is not open to the public, footpaths lead through the grounds down to Lord's Bridge. This was built in 1733 on the site of a ford, the remains of which can still be seen, and from there a signposted footpath follows the river to Redmire. The White Rose Candle factory, which is open to the public, is in a dip below the road in the centre of Wensley and is housed in an old mill. The wheel remains but the wooden leet leading from the waterfall is badly rotted.

Following the decline of Wensley, Leyburn is now regarded as the gateway to the upper reaches of Wensleydale, and on the Friday marked day the town buzzes with activity. The hostelries are frequented by the troops from nearby Catterick, and

97

substantial parts of the surrounding moorlands are fenced off as training areas which abound with wildlife. The river runs through the village which is overlooked from the Shawl, a green area criss-crossed with footpaths and dotted with seats. Nearby is the Queen's Gap where Mary, Queen of Scots, is said to have been recaptured following her escape from Bolton Castle. Apparently she dropped her shawl and thus gave this lovely picnic spot its name. Leyburn lacks an ancient church, for as we have seen it was once governed from Wensley and all it had was a Chapel of Ease. Charles II granted a Tuesday market around 1670 but in 1699 the day was changed to Friday. Despite Wensley having an earlier market, Leyburn can trace its origins back to Domesday when it was called 'Le borne' – a stream by a clearing.

On either side of the Ure and its tributary, the Cover, stand the villages of Spennithorne and East Witton. Spennithorne's Church of St Michael and All Angels was established in Saxon times and many recognisable fragments are incorporated into the present building which dates to 1156. Its main attraction, however, is much more recent. Sebastapol was looted by the British during the Crimean War in 1854. A golden cross which once stood on top of the White Barracks was brought to England by General Sir Charles van Straubenzee who commanded the Light Division. The cross now stands in the churchyard and its gilt reflects every shaft of sunlight. Within the church are several bits of Saxon crosses and a wall painting which came from Jervaulx Abbey. From the church the road descends to a widened packhorse bridge over the Ure. About halfway across and set into a passing spot is a stone which looks like the base of a cross. It may well have been a resting point for coffins being carried to Spennithorne. The views from the bridge and the riverside footpaths are magnificent, and here grow some of the finest-tasting wild gooseberries we ever had the pleasure of bottling, jamming and making into wine.

At the nearby Coverbridge Inn another packhorse bridge spans the Cover which joins the Ure at this point and the road then climbs into East Witton, another fine example of an estate village. The spot is of ancient origin, although it was rebuilt completely along with the church when, in the early nineteenth-century, the Christie family who then owned the

East Witton Church.

Jervaulx estate set about building a model village. Charming cottages, each with a garden, surround a sloping green on which is a stone dated 1859 with a tap set into it – once the village water supply. For those in pursuit of stronger stuff East Witton once had two pubs, the Blue Lion and the Holly Tree which is now a restaurant. The old schoolhouse has been converted into a private dwelling but Rookery Cottage still echoes in the spring to the sound of young birds being fed.

99

Just beyond the village is the Cistercian abbey of Jervaulx, a delightful tangle of ruins, wild and garden plants which is still in private hands. Visiting is allowed on payment into an honesty box. Beneath a sheltering canopy are guidebooks and postcards. There is a free car park, cafe and a craft shop. Jervaulx was founded by accident in 1156, the first abbot being John de Kinston. Whilst en route from Byland Abbey to Foss, John and his twelve companions got lost, and when they entered a wooded valley he had a vision of the Virgin Mary and the child Jesus who said, "Ye are late of Byland but now of Yorevale". The Cistercians remained and called their new abbey Yorevale after the river valley. Later the spelling was altered to the French equivalent – Jervaulx. By the end of the fourteenth-century the abbey owned much of Wensleydale, its wealth depending upon wool, cheese and horses. Although initially made from ewes' milk, Wensleydale cheese has survived the transition to the milk of cows and is still an important part of the economy of the dale. This is also true of horse breeding, and the racing stables which so dominate the little town of Middleham owe their origins to the monks of Jervaulx. Even though the abbey was dissolved around 1540, the spirit of the monks lives on.

We wonder how the Jervaulx monks got on with those from nearby Coverham Abbey which dominated Coverdale, the small tributary of Wenselydale. Just below yet another ancient packhorse bridge is a garden centre which appears to wrap itself around the few, yet very impressive, remains of Coverham Abbey which once had ecclesiastical control of both Coverdale and Kettlewell in Wharfdale. Coverham was not a dominant Cistercian house such as Jervaulx, Rievaulx or especially Fountains, but was a relatively tiny abbey constructed by the Premonstratensian order. Coverham was founded in 1212 and consisted of around twenty canons and rather more lay brethren all under the leadership of an abbot. He also administered churches at Coverham (still standing but closed for worship), Downholme, Kettlewell (where more than 1000 sheep were grazed) and at Sedbergh, plus a rectory at Seaham in Durham. Coverham was never rich and when it was dissolved in 1536 it had a net income of £160,18s 3d. In 1547 the Commissioners of Henry VIII sold the abbey to Humphrey

A unique example of an intact embalming slab near the entrance to Jervaulx Abbey. This was used to preserve the bodies of dignitaries such as abbots. There is a space for the head at one end and a drain for the fluid at the other.

Orme for £419,15s 0d, and the buildings, although ruined, have been in private hands ever since. Many guidebooks indicate that the abbey is not open to the public but the owner of the garden centre allows free access and will even sell you a modestly priced yet informative little guidebook.

We once stayed in Middleham and were awakened on a beautiful May morning by the sound of horses' hooves on cobbles. The sound and sight of horses has been a feature of the town since the days of the monks. There seems to be a stable with its own story to tell of a famous trainer, Derby or National winner along each alleyway leading to a yard. A visit to the 'gallops' on Middleham Moor is a treat for those who are prepared to rise early. There are two areas called Upper and Lower Moors which are still common land and belong to the community charge payers of the town. On their behalf all the trainers pay a fee for each horse into a pool for the privilege of exercising their horses. The local blacksmith told us that each horse has its own made-to-measure shoes, and a spare pair bearing the name of the animal was always waiting to replace a worn set. In contrast to working horses the shoes of racers are always put onto the hoof 'cold'. The normal shoes are of iron, whilst racing plates are made of a special light alloy with an aluminium base. Also in Middleham is a jockeys valet who washes, mends, irons and catalogues the silks and ensures that each rider has a well-polished saddle and boots. This must be just as hard a job as that done by the stable lads who turn out the horses on race day looking immaculate after months of training and hard work on the gallops.

Middleham, said to be Yorkshire's smallest town, has two squares each with its own cross, a castle which was for a brief spell the home of Richard III, and a church which was raised to colliegiate status by that ill-fated and probably much-maligned monarch.

The upper square overlooked by the castle is often called the Swine Cross and according to the plaque on its side is thought 'to commemorate the grant obtained for Middleham in 1479 of a fair and a twice-weekly market at Whitsun week and the feast of St Simon and St Jude by Richard, Duke of Gloucester, later Richard III. The heraldic animal, may be his own cognisance of the White Boar or the emblem of his wife co-heiress of the Lordship of Middleham.' At the side of the Swine Cross is a relatively modern fountain erected to commemorate the accession of Queen Victoria in 1837. Set in the ground nearby is a bull ring. The old school building overlooking the cross was given by James Birch, Rector of Middleham in 1869, and it now serves as an arts workshop.

Before the Normans defeated the Saxons, Middleham belonged to Gilpatric, but in 1069 his birthright was given to Alan the Red, the eldest son of Eudes, the influential Count of Penthievre. He built his own castle overlooking the Swale at Richmond but gave Middleham to his younger brother who bore the now unfortunate name of Ribald. His descendants remained until 1270 when Ralph Fitzranulph failed to provide a male heir, and when his daughter Mary married Robert Neville of Raby the most important chapter in the annals of Middleham began. Over a period of two centuries the Nevilles gained in influence, but as time went on the struggle for power became ever more tangled. Richard Neville, Earl of Salisbury, was beheaded at Pontefract in 1460 and then Richard, Earl of Warwick, more usually referred to as the Kingmaker, was

Jervaulx Abbey is a delightful tangle of stonework and vegetation.

killed during the Battle of Barnet in 1471. Middleham then passed to the crown and Edward IV settled castles and lands on his brother Richard, Duke of Gloucester, the infamous hunchback we know as Richard III. We should ask ourselves three questions: firstly, was Richard actually a hunchback? secondly, was he evil? and thirdly, was Will Shakespeare a liar?

Richard was a small man who had one arm much more highly developed probably due to long training with a bow, but that he was a hunch-back was almost certainly an invention of his Tudor enemies. He was probably implicated in the murder of his brother the Duke of Clarence and his nephews, the Princes in the Tower. Sir Thomas More, anxious to keep in with the reigning Tudors against the Plantagenets, embroidered the history, and Shakespeare also had the political sense to base his plays partly on fact but slanted also to please the Tudor Queen Elizabeth I.

Richard's life and reign were both short – thirty-five and two years respectively – but after he married his cousin Anne Neville who had already been widowed in her teens, he was loved by the locals. Their only son, Edward, was born and died at Middleham and there was no love in the town for Henry VII and the Tudors who took over the area.

It was, however, the first Stuart King, James I, the son of Mary, Queen of Scots, who sold Middleham to Sir Henry Linley in 1604, and when his male line failed the castle and land passed to Edward, Lord Lofthus. His heir sold them to Edward Wood in 1662. Then followed a period of stability until 1889 when Captain Thomas Wood sold the castle to Samuel Cunliffe Lister who eventually became Lord Masham. From 1925 the castle was maintained by the Commissioner of Works and lately by English Heritage which is doing fine interpretative work at Middleham. Displays of falconry are held each Sunday during the season from 2pm and 5pm, weather permitting, and there are also regular Sunday markets.

Richard's benevolent influence can be seen in the church dedicated to St. Alkelda and St. Mary (see Chapter 3). It is said that Middleham's Saxon church was erected over Alkelda's body. When the Norman church which replaced it was being renovated in 1878, female bones of ancient origin were discovered in the altar area. They were reinterred and commemorated by a brass plaque on the most easterly pillar on the south side of the church. Set into the vestry wall are slabs of what are thought to be Saxon masonry and part of the tomb of St. Alkelda.

The first reference to a church is dated 1280 and Mary of Middleham was the patron. She was the last in the line of Ribald and she married Robert Neville; their grandson was a benefactor of religious houses, which included donating the famous Neville Screen to Durham cathedral. In 1340 he enlarged Middleham by moving the south wall of the chancel and nave as well as adding an east window and a clersetory which throws much-needed light into the nave. The sturdy tower was also constructed about this time. The future Richard III would have visited the chantry chapel which was built to ensure rest for the soul of the one-time rector, John Cartmell. It was Richard himself, however, who thrust greatness upon what was merely a typical church of its period. Richard's elder brother, Henry IV, granted him permission to convert the church into a college, thus increasing the number and influence of the clergy employed to run it. A dean and six secular priests offered masses for the souls of the Royal family. In 1482 the Pope approved the foundation by issuing a Papal Bull, and despite Richard's demise the college survived and, even more surprisingly, did not cease to function after the Reformation. It continued until 1845 when an Act of Parliament suppressed all Deaneries but not before Dean Scrimshaw Wood had fought a long legal battle to keep Middleham, a battle which he only finally lost in 1856. One of the last Canons in office was Charles Kingsley who, when he was 26, wrote of Middleham: 'This is quite a racing town. Jockeys and grooms crowd the streets, and I hear they are a most respectable set and many of them regular communicants'.

Our final word on Middleham must concern its bridge, surely the most unusual structure to span the Ure. It is of castellated appearance too narrow to allow vehicles to pass each other, and these days the crossing is controlled by traffic lights. The design was based upon those of the Menai Straits and Conway bridges which were built in 1826. Hansom, designer of the cab, copied the Welsh design with slight variations. The idea was to build castellated pylons with loopholes through which passed cables of iron. Within two years the design had failed. Locals say the bridge collapsed when a herd of cows was crossing and their footsteps fell into unison, setting up vibrations. These shook the bridge until it collapsed! Whatever the reason, a cast-iron carriageway was inserted in 1864 and has worked ever since, but the original castellated towers remain.

Our first visit to Masham brought a feeling of surprise at the size of the market square overlooked by coaching inns, the most impressive being the King's Head with its arched entrance to the old stables at the side. The market cross stands on top of stone steps, once the site of the old stocks, and from these we could look out over the market which, it being Wednesday, was in full swing. We enjoy the hustle and bustle of a market, whether it be human or livestock, but also feel the need for a breath of fresh air, and this lovely old town has a number of tree-lined riverside footpaths. From the square a road leads past the school, down Mill Lane and over a stile into luxuriant water meadows.

Mill Lane does indeed lead to an old mill by the river, and although the water wheel has gone, the building has been beautifully restored as a private residence. Retracing our steps, we looked out over allotments, cricket ground, and spacious car and picnic site to the bridge spanning the Ure. Masham, less than ten miles from Ripon, caters for visitors who love peaceful spots. It also shows us that this is a working countryside, and the town is probably the most important sheep market in the Dales; there is even a Masham breed to underline the point.

Permanent settlement at Masham takes us back at least to Saxon times, and standing outside the church porch is a blackened pillar which formed the base of what must have been a huge cross. It is now badly weather-worn but carvings showing Christ and the Twelve Apostles can still be recognised towards the top, whilst what appear to be lesser saints – perhaps even Paulinus himself – are depicted around the base. A church at Masham is listed in Domesday and some Saxon masonry was no doubt incorporated into the present building begun in 1140. There have been many alterations since, including a fine set of decorated tombs, but all have combined to produce a most fascinating church with a soaring spire overlooking one of the finest market squares in Britain.

During our wanderings around Masham we have been asked many times for directions to the Old Druids' Temple. It comes as something of a shock to discover that this is a modern ruin and a rather good example of a folly, but not very easy to find. Leave Masham on the Swinton Road and then bear left to the village of Ilton. The temple has a car park from which a path leads into Forestry Commission land. The so-called Druids' Temple dates only from the 1820s when the squire of Swinton Hall, William Danby, became distressed at the level of unemployment and decided to provide work at the rate of one shilling (5p) per day, which must have prevented many folk from starving. The structure was an attempt to copy Stonehenge, and when Danby died in 1833 he left a memorial as strange as any in the country.

Masham lies in an angle between the Ure and the River Burn, which is quite a sizeable tributary. Close to one of the feeder streams of the Burn is yet another monument to William Danby, who seems to have led an exciting life. There is a stone shelter, inside which is a seat with a plaque which reads, 'This seat, overlooking some of the beautiful works of the Creator, was built by the grateful mind of William Danby, Esq, A.D. 1832'. The reason for his delight was his release from the hands of Barbary pirates. William must have been a tough and healthy character. He died in 1833 at the age of 81, having become High Sherriff of Yorkshire in 1784.

Just beyond Masham on the Ripon road is West Tanfield with the River Ure flowing beneath a three-arched bridge built in 1734. Attractive cottages lead up from the river, and towering over all is the parish church of St. Nicholas, with a chantry cottage and the remains of a once-mighty Marmion tower – a fifteenth-century gatehouse with an oriel window above a magnificently proportioned arch. This was the home of the Marmion family who first settled here in 1215, the year of Magna Carta. They were made famous in Sir Walter Scott's novel of the same name. The present tower, which is open daily, was built as a fortified house against the invading Scots, and a staircase leads up to the second storey from which there are magnificent views over a valley of trees and down to the river. Inside the church is a superb collection of tombs, including one which may be that of Sir John Marmion who died in 1387 and Lady Elizabeth who passed away in 1400. The wrought-iron surround has prickets for candles which it was customary to light on certain occasions. It is thought to be the only such structure in England. The effigies and tomb are fashioned from Derbyshire alabaster. The Knight is shown wearing fourteenth-century plate armour with his feet resting on a lion and his head supported on a tilting helmet. Strangely for a Yorkshire knight, what is known as a Lancashire collar is shown around his neck. This is an 'SS' shape, a design initiated by Henry IV. The Knight's Lady has her head resting upon a cushion which is supported by angels, whilst her feet rest upon a faithful hound. Embroidered on her kirtle (skirt) are the armorial ensigns of the Marmion and St. Quentin families. Outside the church porch are a set of dog tethers where animals could be left whilst their owners were at prayer. Above one of the tethers is a tombstone set into the wall which is inscribed: 'Here lyeth the body of Ralph Bourn Born Anno 1615 and died in 1728'. He was thus 113 years old!

The Marmions are illuminated by the works of Walter Scott but West Tanfield itself can rightly be said to have lit up the world. In 1871 Miss Elizabeth Clarke of Tanfield Hall married a genius by the name of Colonel Rookes Everly Bell Crompton, who played a vital role in the development of the use of electricity. He set up a waterwheel powered by the Ure and used it to drive a primitive generator which powered the house of his in-laws. Later his house in London was the first to be lit entirely by electricity, and Crompton went on from there to light Buckingham Palace and then Windsor Castle, after which he proceeded to make his fortune by lighting the city of Vienna.

Standing on the bridge and looking over at the swirling waters of the Ure, we wondered if this powerful current had set Crompton thinking. We followed a narrow alleyway overgrown with bramble and other plants which led down to the old ford used before the building of the bridge. Wild garlic was growing in the damp spots along with jack-by-the-hedge which is the food plant for the caterpillars of orange-tip butterflies. The traveller and writer Leland noted in 1530 that he 'crossed the river by ferry for lack of a bridge' and then he proceeded to the church where he mentions 'divers tombs of the Marmion family in a chapel in the North side of the church'. The canopied entrance to this chapel from the interior is still there to this day, but the one-time door to the exterior has been walled up. Leland had an inquisitive mind and would have known that the figure at rest beneath the canopy represents Sir John Marmion who died in 1330, and whose wife Maud founded his chantry chapel, probably in his memory. The female figure in front of Sir John is almost certainly that of Maud herself but the three other figures in the area are somewhat confusing. One, for example, shows a knight in chain mail which could be as early as thirteenth-century. Possibly other members of the family were moved from other parts of the church when the chantry chapel was built. Leland would also have been aware of the esteem in which Thomas Sutton was held. This worthy had been Rector of Tanfield and Canon of Chester, who died in 1492. Just inside the door on the south wall and set into the floor of the choir is a brass plate in memory of his good works.

Middleham Castle.

West Tanfield village is an ideal centre for which to explore the surrounding areas, and visits to Well, Snape and the stone circle at Thornborough are all worthwhile.

Well is a lovely little village divided along the main street by a clear stream. The name derives from the Roman settlement with the largest bathhouse outside Bath itself. There is a medieval legend concerning the Latimer family, a member of which is said to have slain the dragon which prevented access to the essential water supply.

Snape is famous for its privately owned, turreted castle with mullioned windows. Built in medieval times, the castle was substantially altered during the Tudor period, no doubt due to the fact that Catherine Parr, the sixth and the last wife of

Henry VIII, lived here for some years. Just beyond Snape is Thorpe Perror Arboretum which is open from March to November. A friend of ours described as arboretum as a tree zoo, and they are ideal places to visit if you want to learn how to identify the various species. Thorpe Perrow has a number of attractive paths leading through it.

Thornborough Circle is sited just off the road to the right which runs from the village to Snape and West Tanfield. The stones are 4,000 years old and belong to the early Bronze Age.

On the way into Ripon from West Tanfield, on the right-hand side of the road, is Lightwater Valley Theme Park which is attracting an increasing number of visitors. This provides the youngsters with a bit of excitement while their parents are enjoying a peaceful Dales holiday.

The ancient city of Ripon is at the junction of three rivers, the Laver, the Skell and the Ure. It lies on one of the main north-south road routes and in consequence is always a place of hustle and bustle. It does, indeed, earn its reputation as Gateway to the Dales – not only Wensleydale but also Wharfdale, Swaledale and Nidderdale – an impressive list indeed! Beauty surrounds the city, and within it is a great deal of beautifully-proportioned architecture, including a magnificent cathedral.

In the next chapter we shall describe Ripon and its surroundings, leaving the Ure to flow on, towards the Ouse. It passes Ripon racecourse, what is left of Ripon canal, and on to Newby Hall, Aldborough with its extensive Roman remains and Boroughbridge, a Norman development.

CHAPTER 7

Around Ripon

The huge square is the best place to begin a tour of Ripon. The ideal time to start is on Thursday market day, and promptly at eleven o'clock when the Wakeman rings his bell as he has done for centuries. The origins of the office are lost in the mists of time but each year twenty-four of 'his brethren' used to elect him to office. Had he left the town for any reason except the pestilence during his year of office, he was to be fined the sum of £20, a large amount in those days. The Wakeman was an early form of insurance policy. He charged each householder 4 pence if they had a front and back entrance to their dwelling and 2 pence if there was only one entrance. The Town Book, dated 1598, but obviously a copy, tells that the Wakeman 'according to the ancient custome shall cause a horne to be blowne at night during the tyme he is in office, at nyne of the clocke at the foure corners of the crosse in the Market stead, and immediately after to begin his watch, and continue the same till three or foure of the clocke in the morninge. And if it happen any house be broken into on the gatesyde and any goods with drawne out of ye said house ye Wakeman shall make good unto the partie so wronge, in such manner and to such value as shall be determined by a majority of his Brethren'.

Although the Church continued to exert its influence after the reign of Henry VIII, its powers were much reduced and the secular officers gradually demanded more and more power. In 1604 James I granted Ripon its free charter which instructed that the City should be governed by twelve aldermen, twenty-four assistants, two sergeants-at-mace, a clerk and a court of record. A merchant called Hugh Ripley, who was then the elected Wakeman, automatically became the first mayor and the last working Wakeman. The office of Wakeman has been ceremonial ever since. Hugh Ripley's house, which dates back to the fourteenth century, but with seventeenth-century embellishments, stands on the corner of the square and is now used as an Information Centre. There is also a small but impressive local history museum situated within it.

The market square is around two acres in extent and is dominated by an obelisk erected in 1781 by William Aislabie on the site of the old market cross. Until 1880 the market fees were paid to the Church but on receipt of £1,500 their control passed to Ripon Corporation. Shoppers must have wandered the streets of Ripon since the thirteenth century and it would seem that the streets running off the market square have changed little since. Kirkgate, Westgate, Skellgate, Allhallowgate, Stonebridgegate and Saint Agnesgate all take us back to medieval times when streets or 'gates' from the surrounding area led into the market square of Ripon. A Town Trail leaflet can be purchased from the Information Centre and points out a host of fascinating buildings including the twelfth-century chapel of the Hospital of St Mary Magdalen situated in Stonebridgegate. Opposite the Cathedral is the nineteenth-century court house, and there is also the mid-Victorian workhouse in Allhallowgate. The Old Liberty Prison in St Marygate has now been opened as a Prison and Police Museum which is open from May to September each afternoon from Tuesday to Saturday. Despite all this fascinating architecture the centrepiece of Ripon has to be its magnificent Cathedral.

To seek the origins of the Cathedral we must return to seventh-century England and look at the life of St Wilfrid who, as a youth of 19, was described as 'Pleasant in address to all, sagacious in mind, strong in body, swift of foot, ready for any kind of work'. According to the writings of Bede, a group of monks from Melrose led by Abbot Eata arrived at the heathen village of Rhypum to set up a new house. With such men as St Cuthbert, who was a steward, and young Wilfrid how could the venture fail? Wilfrid became the second abbot, and by AD 672 he had raised a fine church described as a 'basilica of polished stone towering to a great height'. Wilfrid employed only the best workers and artists, whilst the collection of bones and other relics ensured a steady stream of pilgrims and, of course, the money they brought with them. Long after his death the Saint's own shrine continued to add to the coffers of Ripon. After the ravages of the Danes, Ripon assumed the

The Wakeman's House in Ripon – now the Information Centre.

role of a collegiate church but this situation was not acceptable to Henry VIII who demanded much more control over his clergy. In 1604, however, James I set up the Ripon charter which restored its status, and this continued until 1836. At that time the diocese of Ripon was organised from the Cathedral.

What remains of the original church in the present structure? Of Wilfrid's church there is little, except a magnificent crypt below the level of the present building, reached on payment of a small fee and then via stone steps from the south side of the nave. The crypt now houses the Cathedral's plate and valuables plus material brought from other churches in the diocese for safe keeping. It would seem that Wilfrid still has the power to add to the church funds! The remains of two early Norman constructions also survive in the undercroft and the chapter house above it. The latter is now used as the library and it was here that the monks were entertained on their way to establish Fountains Abbey. The present church reflects the influence of Roger Pont L'Eveue who was Archbishop of York from 1154 to 1181, a period long enough to allow him time to put his ideas into practice. Seen from any angle, the Cathedral is majestic but the west front is particularly fine. The fourteenth-century east window is among the finest in the land and the soaring arches of the mainly sixteenth-century nave show clearly how often the early buildings collapsed and had to be strengthened and even, at times, rebuilt. Ripon's most impressive feature, however, is the wonderfully carved choir stalls fashioned by craftsmen under the influence of William Bromflet, also named William Carver, who was the Wakeman in 1511. Although a roof fall in 1600 did considerable damage to several canopies which were replaced in the nineteenth century, there was enough medieval work on which the new stalls could be based.

For us it is always something of a wrench to leave the Cathedral which has watched over the Ure valley since the seventh century, but for those with time to spare the nearby Fountains Abbey, one of the finest monastic ruins in Europe, should be savoured on a leisurely visit. By 1132 many monks were beginning to feel that the Benedictine rules of piety were being eroded, and a group of thirteen brothers abandoned life in St Mary's Abbey in York and appealed for land to Archbishop Thurstan at Ripon. They were given a site near the banks of the River Skell, a tributary of the Ure. Under their new Abbot Richard, who had been prior of St Mary's, the monks embraced the more austere Cistercian order. The name 'Fountains' was given to the new abbey because the valley was rich in spring water. To begin with there was much infighting and some skulduggery, which would have been more fitting for scheming medieval politicians than holy men, but eventually peace prevailed. There gradually rose in the valley of the Skell a most remarkable building, and looking at the wonderful setting we see today can lead to the assumption that the monks were given fertile land and all they had to do was build. The truth was quite the reverse because the ground given by Thurstan was said to be 'Thick set by thorns, fit rather to be the lair of wild beasts than human beings'.

Ripon Cathedral.

Visitors to Fountains must pay both a parking and entrance fee and the best approach is via the hauntingly beautiful Fountains Hall, built in 1611 by Sir Stephen Proctor using stone from the dismantled lay brothers' infirmary. Architecturally it would be fair to describe it as a confused building but it does have some fine Jacobean features. It was something of an architectural triumph because the building is set hard into a hillside and has little depth, which may explain why it was provided with five storeys.

We once arrived at Fountains on an Easter Sunday morning just after rain and with a rainbow arching over the ruins. The first rays of sunshine were catching the mist in the valley and giving the impression that the ruins were floating gently on a cloud. Actually the preservation of Fountains owes more to a

The Cellarium at Fountains Abbey – the finest such building in Europe.

'bubble' than to a cloud. John Aislabie inherited Studley Royal Estate, which included the abbey ruins, from his elder brother in 1699. John was the Chancellor of the Exchequer at the time of the South Sea Bubble scandal and was imprisoned in the Tower of London for a short while for what was described as 'infamous foolhardiness and corruption'. Denied an outlet for his energies in public life, John, until his death in 1742, devoted all this time to producing the best possible setting for the abbey ruins which included woodland paths, water gardens, deer park and a Temple of Piety, best viewed when reflected in the waters of a specially constructed canal. These views are best appreciated by visitors entering the area at the northern entrance, from which a winding path leads down through Studley Royal estate to the abbey ruins. These are seen at their best in late summer and early autumn when, as night closes in, they are floodlit. The most impressive part is the 302-foot (92m) long *cellarium* which runs southwards from the nave of the church to the river. When this was repaired recently great care was taken to cause minimal disturbance to the colonies of

Fountains Abbey – the finest ruin in Britain, undergoing restoration.

long-eared and pipistrelle bats which are now protected by law. Although it is now open at both ends, the *cellarium*, the ceiling of which is supported by nineteen huge pillars, seems once to have been divided into five storerooms by means of wooden partitions.

We wonder what business was done here and if it involved trading in wool, for which Fountains was famous throughout Europe. The cellarer was the monk in charge of storing the wool, and may well have had to show his European visitors around the vaulted *cellarium*. Perhaps it was built in such a grand style in much the same way that modern boardrooms are built and furnished to impress potential buyers. By the fourteenth century the monastic wool trade was England's most important industry and Fountains, with an output of 27,664 pounds (12,350 kg), was by far the largest producer although Easby in Swaledale and Jervaulx in Wensleydale were also important.

When Henry VIII dissolved Fountains in 1539 he made a

large amount of money from its sale, and like many other religious houses it was used as an unofficial quarry, as Fountains Hall bears impressive witness. We must thank the South Sea Bubble that the Abbey's decline into obscurity was arrested. Fountains Abbey is administered by the National Trust and is open daily except Christmas Day and Boxing Day. Guided tours are available and special events include floodlit evenings, occasional performances of Shakespeare's plays, and what is delightfully called 'Music by Moonlight'.

Harrogate, strictly speaking, is not part of the Dales, but it caters so well for tourists, especially those heading for Wensleydale and Nidderdale, that it needs to be considered. A relatively modern town close to Knaresborough, Harrogate began as a spa town but has now adapted itself to become one of the most important conference and trade fair centres in Britain. There is an International Conference Super Centre with an attached banqueting hall. This modern architecture fits well into the nineteenth-century complex of solid-looking hotels built to cater for those who came to take the waters and breathe in the bracing air. Genteel teashops and exotic confectionary are still the hallmark of the town, and many of the hotels have retained a Victorian atmosphere, whilst others were built during the coaching days.

The health-giving mineral springs were perhaps known to St Mungo in the sixth century but were first utilised in 1571 by William Slingsby who had sampled European waters, and over his first well on the site a temple-like building has been erected. At first there were no exotic buildings but visitors simply bathed in the water itself or barrels of it were delivered to the inns. The Royal Pump Room, which was built in 1842, is now open to the public as a museum of local history and costume, but it is still possible to sample the sulphur-tainted water from the old well. Once the railway came to Harrogate and provided a link with the properous south and also the woollen areas of Leeds and Bradford, the town developed quickly. The Royal Baths Assembly Rooms still have the original ornately tiled Turkish baths but there are also up-to-date saunas and a *solarium*. To view the town at its best, climb up to Harlow Hill with its observatory tower built in 1829.

Close to the town in the Nidd Valley is the Darley Mill

Centre which houses an exhibition about corn milling. The mill wheel and race of the thirteenth-century building have been restored and there is an excellent cafe and restaurant which usually has a roaring fire in winter. There are also bargains to be found in linen and woollen ware plus other gifts and crafts.

Obviously because of its relatively recent development Harrogate has no castle or ancient church and was once a hamlet on the outskirts of Knaresborough which is the 'Gateway to Nidderdale'.

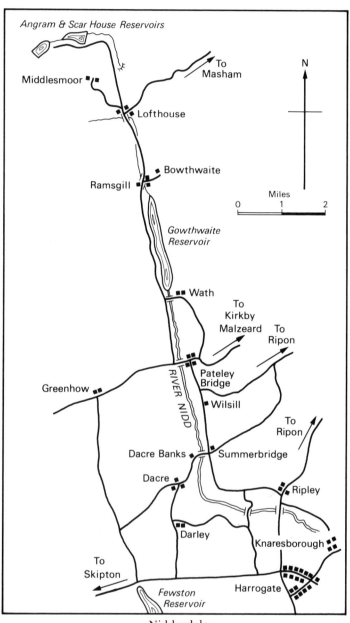

Nidderdale.

CHAPTER 8

Nidderdale

Nidderdale is unique because it is the only Yorkshire Dale which, unless one is a mountaineer, can only be entered from one end. This cul-de-sac has therefore retained its sense of wildness. The upper reaches of the River Nidd are dominated by the bulk of Great Whernside (2310 feet – 703 metres) and Little Whernside (1984 feet – 604 metres). Neither should be confused with Whernside, which overlooks Ribblesdale above Settle. The word 'whern' is thought to derive from 'quern', which was a hollowed stone used to grind corn. These hand tools were the forerunners of the millwheels which were also made of the millstone grit which caps the local limestone.

The river issuing from Nidd Head finally reaches the sea via the Ouse which it joins and Nun Monkton, a charming village about seven miles from York. Nidderdale is best explored by using Knaresborough, or perhaps Harrogate, as a base, travelling to Ripley and then on to Pateley Bridge via Brimham Rocks. Pateley Bridge is the perfect centre for discovering Upper Nidderdale.

Knaresborough derives its name from the Anglo-Saxon Knarres-burg which means the fortress on the rock. Perched on a bluff of sandstone about 100 feet (30 metres) above the River Nidd, it was easily defended and the Brigantes had a fort there. It is more than likely that the Romans would have taken over the site and constructed a small fort close to the York road. It was with the coming of the Normans, however, that the history of Knaresborough really began.

The hustle and bustle of the Wednesday market can make parking a problem, but on other days there is space available in the square providing a free disc is obtained from local shops. Few market places are able to compete with Knaresborough and there has probably been a market on this site since it provisioned the castle way back in Norman times. Edward II granted the first *official* charter in 1310, and when Leland visited the town in the late sixteenth century he wrote that 'the market there is quick', by which he meant lively. We know just what he meant and we love to arrive early on a Wednesday to watch street traders setting up their stalls, hemmed in but also sheltered by Tudor and Georgian shops. During the eighteenth century Knaresborough was reputed to be the most important corn market in Yorkshire. Here is the oldest chemist's shop in England which was established as an apothecary's in 1720. The interior is a joy, with low oak-beamed ceilings, antique bottles and dark drawers labelled in old gilt lettering. Fortunately the shop has a modern dispensary but few can resist looking at the couch on which patients were bled and also the spot where primitive dentistry was practised. The Lawrence family were chemists here for around a century before W.P. Lawrence retired in 1965. No new visitor to the shop should leave without a sweet-smelling bottle of Old English Lavender Water which is made from a recipe handed down since the eighteenth century.

From the square it is but a gentle stroll to the ruins of the castle, the building of which began soon after the Norman Conquest when William rewarded Serlo de Burgh, who had fought with him at Hastings in 1066, with a sizeable area of land in the north of the Kingdom. Despite this early start the bulk of the ruins date to the fourteenth century. Knaresborough, however, was associated with one of the most dastardly deeds in English history – the murder of Thomas à Becket. After they had rid their king of the upstart priest the four knights found their master to be ungrateful and in 1170 they fled to Knaresbourough in an unsuccessful effort to escape punishment. King John of Magna Carta (1215) fame used the castle as his base when hunting in Knaresborough Forest. Edward III also liked the castle and came here with Queen Philippa and their two sons – the Black Prince and John of Gaunt. At one time Knaresbourough belonged to the de Burgh family but they backed Simon de Montfort's rebellion against Henry III and the King confiscated their lands.

When John of Gaunt, Duke of Lancaster, was given the castle in 1372 there began a link with the Duchy which continues to this day. The Queen is officially the Duke of Lancaster and she therefore owns the castle. Within the grounds are lovely gardens, a bowling green and a museum. Before its destruction

Knaresborough Market Square.

during the civil wars of the 1640s the castle had its share of important occupants. Thomas Chaucer, son of the poet, was constable at Knaresborough and Richard II was imprisoned here before being taken to Pontefract Castle where he was murdered. In its heyday when John of Gaunt rode through the gates the castle had twelve large towers and a massive keep, the upper storey of which became known as the King's Chamber from the day Richard II left it to go to his death:

> And to Knaresburg after led was he.
> But to Pontefracte last, where he did dee.

The view from the ramparts down to the Nidd must have been breathtakingly beautiful. The view today, despite the intrusion of a railway viaduct – which is surprisingly majestic – is still one of the finest in the country. When Cromwell's men destroyed the castle they left the courtroom standing, and a careful look at this will reveal its base to be fourteenth century. The upper sections were added between 1590 and 1600 at the expense of Sir Henry Slingsby. The building is now a museum open mainly during the summer months and depicts the history of the town and the castle. Our favourite section deals with the old characters of the town including Blind Jack and Mother Shipton.

John Metcalfe was born in 1717, died in 1810 and for all but six of these years he was blind following an attack of smallpox. Despite this handicap he proved to be a most accomplished horseman and a fine musician, the latter skill being much more understandable. He played the fiddle at the newly developing Spa at nearby Harrogate and was also the musician to the Knaresborough Volunteers who battled against Bonnie Prince Charlie in 1745. 'Blind Jack' was an astute businessman, operating his own stagecoach, and was a reliable carrier of all sorts of merchandise. Small wonder he was concerned at the state of eighteenth-century roads, and this is why he became one of the most skilful constructors of turnpike roads in the country. Much of his work can still be seen in the Yorkshire Dales and in Lancashire. The museum has on display Blind Jack's viameter, which is a wheel he used to measure distances.

With Mother Shipton we have fewer facts to go on, which has given writers something of a free hand. She is said to have been born in a cave around 1488 to an unmarried girl. This was close to the dropping well which we will describe later. Despite being particularly ugly she married Toby Shipton of York and began to gain fame because of her prophecies. She is said to have predicted that Cardinal Wolsey was heading for a fall and would never become the Archbishop of York, which was regarded as the last rung on the ladder to Canterbury. In this she was right but her long-term predictions were mixed, and there is some evidence that a nineteenth-century bookseller from Brighton deleted some inaccurate forecasts whilst allowing others to stand. Among these were predictions that there would be machines which could fly, the bridge over the Nidd would collapse, and the end of the world would come. We do have aeroplanes, on 11th March 1848 the first railway viaduct over the Nidd collapsed, but the world is still with us. Two out of three isn't bad!

From the castle there are several routes down to the river, the most historic being Water Bag Bank. This was the town's only water supply until 1764 when a pump was installed below the castle. The water was carried in leather bags up the steep bank either by donkey or horse. The only opposition came

The Court House in Knaresborough Castle, now a museum.

from local women who carried up buckets of water at a halfpenny a load.

The Nidd is deep and tranquil at Knaresborough and boats can be hired close to the road bridge. Those who want to stretch their legs can pay an entry fee at a gate on the opposite bank of the river near the High Bridge and follow the path via the Dropping Well to the Low Bridge. Some prefer to take their cars through the gate and make use of the picnic site. The High Bridge is of ancient origin but was substantially enlarged in 1773, when it was known as Danyell Bridge. In 1924 another strengthening was required and it now carries an almost endless stream of traffic on the way to York and Harrogate. The paths through the Dropping Well estate were first laid out by the Slingsby family between 1738 and 1740. About halfway between the viaduct and the famous well is a tumbling weir which can be heard long before it is seen. This once powered the Castle Mill which can be seen on the opposite bank. It was originally constructed as a cotton mill in 1791, but was soon converted to flax. At its peak the mill produced 20,000 yards of linen each week and the product was so highly regarded that Waltons Mill supplied royalty. Weaving continued until 1972 and in 1984 Harrogate District Council purchased the mill.

The walk continues along the line followed in 1540 by John Leland who described 'A welle of a wonderful nature caullid Droping Welle. For out of the great Rokkes by it distilleth water continually into it . . . what thing so ever ys caste in, or growith about the Rokke and is touched of this water, groweth into stone'. It is significant that at this time Leland does not refer to Mother Shipton, or the cave of her birth situated just behind the well, nor does he mention the Wishing Well, but his description of the Dropping Well is very accurate. The impregnation works best on soft porous objects such as gloves and small woolly objects. The last time we were there, there were a couple of grinning Garfield cats waiting to be 'done' in the stream of water which tumbles over the rocks at a rate calculated at around 700 gallons per hour. In order to keep the well functioning in a controlled manner the deposits are scraped off the overhanging rock, otherwise it could become top heavy and a potential danger to visitors. Towards the end of the walk at Low Bridge there is a lovely avenue of graceful beeches seen at their best in autumn. Eventually the woodland gives way to the road crossing Low Bridge, which once carried the main road into Knaresborough before Harrogate developed. The old name for the structure was March Bridge – march meaning a boundary. Looking over the bridge, it is possible to see the line of the old ford which it was built to replace, and a substantial enlargement took place in 1799. Anyone wanting to see the ford at close quarters should visit the area on Boxing Day because since 1968 a tug of war has taken place between muscular heavyweights representing the Half Moon and Mother Shipton's Inn which lie on either side of the Nidd. The losers are dragged through the ford.

Just down Abbey Road is the House in the Rock and the Chapel of our Lady of the Crag. Why Abbey Road? At one time there was a Trinitarian Priory dedicated to St Robert which probably began its ministry in the middle of the thirteenth century. Apparently St Robert had a reputation as a skilled herbalist, so Knaresborough's pharmacy is even older than the shop! St Robert lived at first in a cave near Grimbald Bridge. His followers, the Trinitarian Friars, did excellent work in begging for money which was used to pay the ransoms of knights held hostage by the Saracens during the Crusades. The

The railway viaduct and River Nidd at Knaresborough.

later friars would have known the shrine cut out of solid rock by John the Mason in 1410, also known as the Chapel of Our Lady of the Crag. The carved figure apparently guarding the entrance is probably not that of St Robert, but of a Knight Templar, since this order had a training ground at the nearby village of Little Ribston. In contrast the House in the Rock is something of a folly hacked out of the rock by a weaver named Thomas Hill and his son of the same name. From 1770 they laboured for eight years to produce a house which they first called Swallow's Nest, but gradually a more pretentious attitude developed and the name was changed to Fort Montague. The owners assumed the title of Sir Thomas Hill and flew a flag outside their residence as well as firing the occasional salute from their battlements.

Before leaving Knaresborough, some time should be spent in and around the parish church of St John the Baptist. Building commenced around AD 1100 using magnesian limestone from local quarries. Some evidence of this early Norman building is seen in the foundations of the tower and also in some chevron 'string' carving on the east side of the church. The tower is mainly late twelfth-century but the spire sprouting from the centre like a pot plant is sixteenth-century. To call this arrangement unique would be wrong, but it is unusual in the

North of England although the practice was more common
further south and is known as a Hertfordshire Spike. On a
lovely June Tuesday evening we looked into the pink sky of the
setting sun and heard the peal of eight bells which have rung
out since 1774. The tradition of ringing the church bells on the
night before market day goes back to medieval times when they
guided visitors through the Forest of Knaresborough. The
tower also has a sundial, a clock and an inscription which tells
us that they are 'redeeming the time'. If there's one thing you
can't afford to waste in Knaresbourgh it is time – there is so
much to see. The gems of St John's are the font and two fine
chapels, one dating to the twelfth century and the other a
reminder of the Slingsby family who dominated
Knaresborough for centuries. The font is Tudor, probably
fashioned in stone during the Perpendicular period of
architecture, the time when the nave was largely remodelled.
The cover is of finely carved wood and dates from around
1685. Why did fonts need a cover? There was a trend which
began in the Middle Ages to steal holy water and use it in
witchcraft, or to sell it to herbalists.

To the right of the altar is a graceful Early English arch
dating to the late twelfth century and leading into St Edmund's
Chapel. This has had its share of Royal patronage, including
that of King John who rode in great ceremony down to the
church from the castle before setting out to hunt in the forest.
The real glory of the chapel, however, dates from 1343 when
Queen Phillipa, wife of Edward III, restored it after it had
been badly damaged in 1318 during a Scots raid.

The Slingsby Chapel has been described as dark and
oppressive – we would prefer to call it stark but impressive. It is
a record of the history of Knaresborough, since the family
dominated its fortunes from 1333 until 1869 when Sir Charles
Slingsby was drowned near Newby Hall during a fox hunt
when he tried to cross the River Ure. The largest and oldest of
the tombs is dated 1601 and commemorates the lives of Francis
and Mary Slingsby, the two depicted lying in state side by side.
Henry, their son, who died in 1634, is shown rising from the
dead whilst another son, William, who passed away in the same
year, is depicted standing with one arm on his shield and his
elbow resting on the hilt of his sword. One member of the

Knaresborough Parish Church.

family who is not commemorated is their uncle William Slingsby who discovered the Tewit (Tewit is a local name for a lapwing) Well in 1571 which he named a Spa after the Belgian town which also marketed spring water.

The Slingsby with most claim to a place in history, however, is Sir Henry who was such a staunch Royalist that it cost him his life. He fought bravely at Marston Moor and was a founder member of the Royalist Secret Society called the Sealed Knot. He was beheaded on the orders of Cromwell in 1658 and his headless body now lies beneath a black marble slab brought from St Robert's Priory.

In the Middle Ages the church and education were closely interlinked, and the long grey building at the top of the churchyard was once King James's Grammar School, founded in 1616, in which 'The maister shall have diligent regard to his scholars and see that they come not uncombed, unwashed, ragged or slovenly'. The present building dates from 1741, and it continued in use until 1901 when the school moved to its present site off York Road. Modern scholars would not be pleased if they had to follow the rules of the old school. In the summer, lessons began at 6 a.m. but in winter they could be lazy and lie in until 7 a.m. The boys were expected to provide their own paper, pens and ink as well as candles. An even stranger rule was that they had to provide their own bow and arrows and were expected to practise. We wonder how many of the old boys stood as soldiers during the siege of the castle or on the bloody battlefield at Marston Moor. They must have wished they had worked harder during their games periods. The school first admitted girls in 1893 and became comprehensive in 1971 but has retained links with King James, and the badge incorporates his tartan.

The most historic route into Nidderdale from Knaresbourough is via Ripley and Brimham Rocks to Pateley Bridge. Probably because of its church, Ripley looks older than it really is since the village was remodelled in 1827 on the lines of a French village typical of the Alsace-Lorraine region. One building is inscribed 'Hotel de Ville', but true Yorkshire grit is seen in the stone, the cobbled square, the market cross and the stocks, not to mention the church and the castle, which has long been the home of the Ingilby family. They were granted land here when Thomas Ingilby saved King Edward III when he was attacked by a wild boar whilst hunting in the forest. Most of their castle dates from the fifteenth century and it is open to the public. Its most attractive features are lavishly decorated rooms and a secret hiding place, a reminder of the days when Catholics were persecuted and often needed to conceal their priests. The grounds are a delight with lakes and gardens designed by Capability Brown. All Saints' Church is mainly fourteenth century and contains many memorials to the Ingilby family. Not so pleasant are the memorials said to have been left by Cromwell's troops in the form of bullet holes in the stone. Several Ripley men who had fought at Marston Moor were lined up against the wall and shot. Close to the church is the so-called Weeping Cross, the only one of its kind in Yorkshire. There are holes in the base of the cross into which it is said pilgrims or sinners could push their knees whilst paying homage at the cross itself.

Brimham Rocks certainly look man-made and religious but in fact are neither, being one of the most haunting geological formations to be found anywhere in the world. We have never met anyone who was not profoundly affected by Brimham

The Slingsby Tomb in Knaresborough Church.

Rocks, huge sandstone structures formed in desert conditions around 300 million years ago. Worn by wind and rain into truly fantastic shapes, the rocks have been given equllay fantastic names including Indian's Turban, Baboon's Head, the Sphinx, Dancing Bear, the Blacksmith and his Anvil, Druid's cave and the Druid's Writing Desk. When visitors began exploring this heather-clad area, the legend grew that they had been carved by the Druids. There are well-marked paths running among the rocks, and next to one called the Crocodile is Brimham House, now an Information Centre in which the local geology is explained. The 145-hectare (362 acre) site is owned by the National Trust who have provided plenty of car parking space on payment of a modest fee. From the Trig Point near Brimham House, 987 feet (301 metres) above sea level, there are splendid views, as well as many a stiff breeze. On a clear day one can see the Humber estuary, and York Minster can easily be picked out.

Pateley Bridge is the only route into Upper Nidderdale, but it has beauty of its own, and the small villages which surround it are all well worth exploring. Tourists are well catered for and there are a number of well-appointed caravan sites. The Nidderdale Museum was opened in 1975. Run by local enthusiasts, it occupies part of the former council offices opposite the parish church. Here all aspects of local life are illustrated and there is a room set up as a Victorian parlour and another as a cobbler's shop. It is worth the small admission fee just to talk to the enthusiastic part-time staff who obviously love Nidderdale. The museum is open every Sunday afternoon and on each afternoon during the summer but also at other times by appointment.

The name Pateley may derive from Pate, which is the old name for a badger, or perhaps from Patleia which means a path through the glade and which was first mentioned in the twelfth-century. Originally the main village was set high on the hillside near the ruined fourteenth-century church of St Mary which was damaged during the Scots raids around 1318. In 1320 a market and a fair to be held on the Feast of St Mary was granted. Alas, this market has lapsed but the Feast, the first Monday after 17th September, is now the date of the Nidderdale Show, and the highlight of the year. St Mary's Church is reached via a set of steps to the right and at the top of the sloping High Street, and the path leads on to Panorama Walk. Nearby is Yorke's Folly, a pair of towers paid for by the Yorke family to provide work for the destitute at the end of the Napoleonic wars. There were originally three towers but one blew down in 1893.

The present parish church, built in the nineteenth-century, is dedicated to St Cuthbert but it does have on view a bell brought to the town when Fountains Abbey was dissolved in the late 1530s. This now has a place of honour in the body of the church and its Latin inscriptions are clearly legible.

A bridge at Pateley is first mentioned in 1320 but this would have been made of wood, the present structure being built in the eighteenth-century but subsequently widened on the upstream side. Beyond it is a pleasant little park with a children's playground, tennis courts and bowling greens lending it an almost seaside atmosphere.

There is plenty of accommodation, making Pateley Bridge an ideal centre from which to explore the Stump Cross Caverns

Brimham Rocks – natural rocks which look like ancient statues.

133

and a cluster of pretty little villages. The town itself is the starting point for a trip into Upper Nidderdale. To reach Stump Cross involves a very steep climb to Greenhow which was a centre of lead mining from Roman times. On Hayshaw Bank near the village two 'pigs' of lead were found dated from AD 81 and inscribed IMP CAES DOMITIANO AUG, COS VII, and one of these is on display at Ripley Castle. The value of the mines was realised by the monks of both Fountains and Byland abbeys and the riches were disputed by the two houses in 1226. Between 1363 and 1365 Nidderdale lead was exported as far afield as Windsor Castle where it was used for roofing. The mines were worked until the end of the nineteenth-century, and more recent attempts to have them re-opened have failed. Just beyond Greenhow on the way to Grassington are the Stump Cross Caverns by the side of the road which links Nidderdale with Wharfedale.

The limestone caves are open daily from Easter to November from 10.00am to 5.30pm and on winter Sundays from 11am to 4pm. There is ample parking, an information centre, a cafe and a shop from which books, postcards, rock samples and jewellery can be purchased. The underground system, reached via steps from the paybox, is lit by electricity and is a narrow twisting passage full of unusual rock formations. These have been named according to shape and there is the jewel box, the snowdrifts, the hawk, the world-famous sentinel, the chamber of pillars, the cradle, the sandcastles, the policeman's truncheon, the organ, the sleeping cat, the cathedral, and right at the end of the system, the wedding cake. On the return journey a fork to the right leads into the Wolverine Cave in which the bones of bison, reindeer, wolf and, of course, the wolverine itself have been found plus a wide variety of mammals still present in the area such as the badger and the fox. Experts from the Natural History Museum in London have dated the finds to between 35,000 and 200,000 years ago. The wolverine interested the scientists who pointed out that the vicious carnivore, a member of the weasel family, which still survives in Scandinavia, Canada and the USSR, is seldom found as a fossil in Britain and has been extinct here for many thousands of years. Bones, when exposed to the elements out in the open, decay quickly, but within a limestone cave they are

Stump Cross Caverns.

protected and the alkaline conditions prevailing are perfect for preservation.

The exploration of Stump Cross Caverns has been going on since the lead miners from Greenhow broke into the network in 1858. Prospecting has been going on ever since, but no significant deposits of lead have ever been discovered. For this we visitors should be grateful because commercial mining would certainly have taken little account of anything of scientific interest. The derivation of the name Stump Cross is of interest. Originally there may have been two crosses called 'Craven' and 'Stub' which probably marked estate boundaries. Their precise position is not known now but presumably 'Stub' cross was close to the present visitor centre.

Smelthouses is yet another now attractive hamlet which had connections with the processing of lead ore. The monks of Fountains Abbey established a smelting mill here around 1350 and ore was brought to it from Greenhow across the Nidd at Lead Wath. The now quiet road through the village was on one of Blind Jack's turnpike routes to Knaresborough, but was replaced in 1827 by a New Line through to Summerbridge. The old monks road can also still be seen running parallel to the Smelthouses road and is now a well-used bridle path. The turnpike was routed through Smelthouses because here was Thomas and Henry Kirkby's flax mill, the earliest such factory in Nidderdale, which was established in 1798. Little Mills was also originally a flax mill but in the 1840s changed to the production of bobbins, and Knox Manor Restaurant was yet another flax mill.

Glasshouses is an example of an industrial village having developed because of a philanthropic family of owners. It is reached from Pateley Bridge along a riverside footpath of around a mile. The first mention of the village is in 1387, but apart from a few isolated farm and handloom weavers' cottages little seems to have happened until 1828 when John and George Metcalfe who were also brewers transferred their then small flax-making business to Glasshouses. In a short space of time they altered the appearance of the village by constructing a reservoir to ensure a reliable water supply to drive a 32-foot diameter wheel to power the machinery. They built houses and amenities for their workers, and George Metcalfe Junior carried on the good work. He it was who brought the North Eastern railway to Pateley Bridge in 1862. He also built himself Castlestead Mansion close to the weir, but after George died the Metcalfe business declined, the village remaining as their memorial.

The energetic can walk up the valley from Pateley Bridge by

The picnic site and dam at Scar House.

following the Nidderdale Way, whilst motorists follow the narrow but usually quiet road. The whole area is so beautiful that it has been called 'Yorkshire's Lake District' and also 'Little Switzerland'. Just beyond Pateley Bridge is the Water Mill Inn which was once the Foster Beck Flax Mill built around 1800. The 34-foot diameter overshot waterwheel was one of the largest in the country and was still working in 1967. The building and the wheel were both renovated in 1990 and the inn has developed a reputation for restaurant meals and bar snacks. There is a garden and a play area for children. The mill lodges at the rear have been stocked with trout and day tickets are available to anglers.

Just beyond the inn a tiny packhorse bridge to the right of the main road leads to the hamlet of Wath. Here is a private house which was once a station on the Nidd Valley Railway. Why should a railway be cut a distance of thirteen miles into the wildest areas of Upper Nidderdale? The answer is water. As Bradford expanded its industries during the nineteenth-century, it became ever more thirsty. In the 1890s permission was obtained to construct reservoirs at Angram and Scar House just downstream from the source of the Nidd. The valley was so remote that no road was available to transport men and materials. The line was unique in Britain since it was the only example of a passenger-carrying railway built and operated by a municipality. Construction began on July 13th 1904 and the line was opened by the Lord Mayor of Bradford on September 11th 1907. There were four stations along the line and since the closure in 1964 the buildings have been converted into private houses. Apart from Wath our favourite is at Lofthouse where the old station is now a bookshop which also sells plants.

At one time the Nidd must have meandered between Wath and Ramsgill but the valley is now flooded by the two-mile length of Gouthwaite reservoir, completed in 1901 and the last of the trio of Bradford's reservoirs but only used as compensation water for the two higher up the valley. Part of Gouthwaite has now been set aside as a nature reserve and this means that Nidderdale is an ideal place for a winter visit; there are many species of wildflowl including Canada geese, pochard, tufted duck, goosanders and mallard. Rarities occur here more frequently than on most waters, and here we have watched pied billed grebe, red necked grebe and Slavonian grebes.

Ramsgill is a splendidly cosy little hamlet dominated by the ivy-clad Yorke Arms, once a shooting lodge, overlooking a perfect English village green. Next to the inn is a cottage, once a school, which was in operation in 1833 and had twenty-five fee-paying students but also offered seven free places. Although the church dates only from 1842, there is an interesting structure nearby. This is the gable end of a chapel built by the monks of Byland Abbey who had a grange (farm) here. Beyond Ramsgill is Lofthouse which, so far as the local 'bus service is concerned, is the head of Nidderdale. In this case where is the river? This is true limestone country and the river goes underground into a swallowhole – called for some unexplained reason Manchester Hole – near Beggarmote Scar and emerges near the old vicarage at Nidd Heads. The dry valley can be followed and runs close to the modern road. Nearby Goyden Pot's Mouth is some nine feet high (0.9m), and this swallows some of the overflow water when Manchester Hole is unable to cope with the volume of water.

Just above this area are the two reservoirs at Scar House and Angram which were at one time remote areas. Access to them was difficult, and a permit was needed. A more realistic attitude now prevails and the Yorkshire Water Authority (Western Division) encourage visitors to drive along the road to the reservoirs on payment of a small fee. There is a pay and display meter at the entrance but coaches, caravans and motor

Scar House Shanty Town shops (above). A locomotive waits for a load of cement (below).

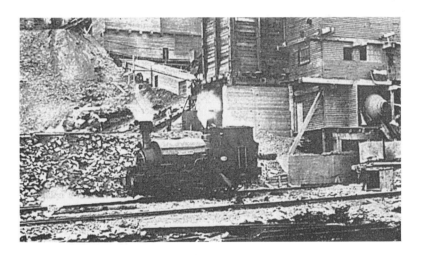

How Stean Gorge Cafe.

cycles are prohibited. The area is open all the year round from 10am to 9pm or dusk, whichever is the earlier. The most interesting features are the dams of the two reservoirs which, when they were built, were the largest such structures in Britain. Scar House dam is 1800 feet (549 metres) long, 170 feet (52 metres) high and at the base is 135 feet (41 metres) thick. Both are a tribute to the work of the 700 men who lived here, some with their families, in a shanty town which has long since vanished. It is hard to believe that the navvies had cinema, church, concert hall, a writing room and even tennis courts. The stone was quarried from the nearby hillside and the quarry sites have now been converted into small car parks and picnic areas. Although all traces of the shanty town have gone, there is one reminder of an even earlier age. This is known as the Lodge and from its ruins radiate the old packhorse tracks which traversed the ancient forest of Knaresborough. One important track came out of Coverdale and was thus a link into Wensleydale and touches Dead Man's Hill. This is said to take its name from Maggie Thompson's evil deeds. Although these grizzly events took place more than 200 years ago, there is some proof that she murdered three Scots pedlars for their money and had their bodies carried up into the hills to be buried. Proof was lacking for many years after her death until peat diggers unearthed their bodies on Dead

Man's Hill – retrospective but fairly damning evidence.

A short way updale past the turn-off to the reservoirs is a sign to How Stean Gill which all the guidebooks describe as a miniature Grand Canyon. We feel that this somehow steals some of the glory from one of the most impressive geological sites in Britain. A small payment is required to walk through the gill, but there is free parking, a shop and a cafe specialising in homemade food. Once more motor cyclists are not welcome but the field behind is popular with campers. Some care must be taken when walking through the gorge which is spanned by a number of rustic bridges, and special vigilance is needed after rain or during frost. Like any combination of rock and water, however, How Stean is seen to best effect after a downpour or when hanging with icicles. The management stresses the dangers and one can even hire strong torches from the cafe. Tom Taylor's Cave is the highlight of the system and is named after the highwayman who lurked here in safety between 'business trips'. Steps lead into and out of the vast cave which is 530 feet (162 metres) long, and it was here in 1868 that two boys found thirty-two Roman coins on a ledge. These are now on display at York Museum. Another treasure is the 170-foot (52m) long How Stean Tunnel which runs along the stream bed and under the road. This is limestone country at its best, but don't forget to take strong shoes and a torch.

The whole of Upper Nidderdale is fine and occasionally tough walking country but one of our favourite easy strolls runs from How Stean to the little village of Middlesmoor, the highest settlement in the Dale. It is dominated by the parish church of St Chad set high on a hilltop. There has been a church here for more than a thousand years, but the present building was only erected in 1866, although some of the ancient stones were obviously re-used. It is inside, however, that we find the real treasure. St Chad's Cross is said to date from around AD 665 when the holy man who became Bishop of Ripon preached here.

Our final and definitive view of Nidderdale has to be from Middlesmoor churchyard where seats have been placed to take full advantage of the site. It really does look like the Lake District even if its geology is different. Here are hills capped with millstone grit contrasting sharply with the limestone of the

The Celtic Cross at Middlesmoor dedicated to St Chad is one of the most important artefacts in Britain.

lower slopes and valley bottoms. For lovers of the Dales, Upper Nidderdale has to be the wildest and most fascinating, but as the Duke of Wellington said in a different context – It is a damned close-run thing. What about Swaledale, for example?

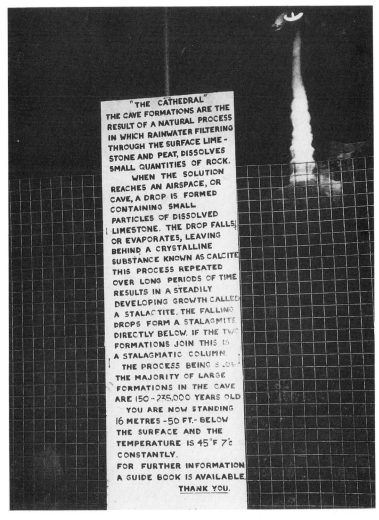

"THE CATHEDRAL"
THE CAVE FORMATIONS ARE THE
RESULT OF A NATURAL PROCESS
IN WHICH RAINWATER FILTERING
THROUGH THE SURFACE LIME -
STONE AND PEAT, DISSOLVES
SMALL QUANTITIES OF ROCK.
WHEN THE SOLUTION
REACHES AN AIRSPACE, OR
CAVE, A DROP IS FORMED
CONTAINING SMALL
PARTICLES OF DISSOLVED
LIMESTONE. THE DROP FALLS
OR EVAPORATES, LEAVING
BEHIND A CRYSTALLINE
SUBSTANCE KNOWN AS CALCITE
THIS PROCESS REPEATED
OVER LONG PERIODS OF TIME
RESULTS IN A STEADILY
DEVELOPING GROWTH CALLED
A STALACTITE. THE FALLING
DROPS FORM A STALAGMITE
DIRECTLY BELOW. IF THE TWO
FORMATIONS JOIN THIS IS
A STALAGMATIC COLUMN.
THE PROCESS BEING SLOW
THE MAJORITY OF LARGE
FORMATIONS IN THE CAVE
ARE 150 - 235,000 YEARS OLD
YOU ARE NOW STANDING
16 METRES - 50 FT.- BELOW
THE SURFACE AND THE
TEMPERATURE IS 45°F 7°c
CONSTANTLY.
FOR FURTHER INFORMATION
A GUIDE BOOK IS AVAILABLE.
THANK YOU.

Notice at Stump Cross Caverns explaining how the area was formed.

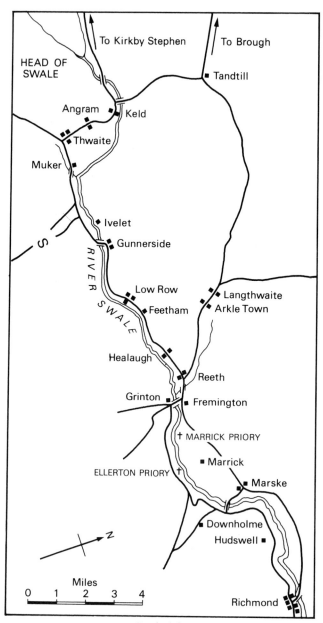

To Kirkby Stephen

To Brough

HEAD OF
SWALE

■ Tandtill

■ Angram   ■ Keld

■■ Thwaite

Muker ■

■ Ivelet

■ Gunnerside

■ Low Row   ■ Langthwaite
■ Feetham   ■ Arkle Town

Healaugh ■

■ Reeth

Grinton ■   ■ Fremington

† MARRICK PRIORY

■ Marrick

ELLERTON PRIORY †   ■ Marske

■ Downholme
Hudswell ■

N

Miles

0 1 2 3 4

Richmond ■■

Swaledale.

CHAPTER 9

Swaledale

The old market town of Richmond is rightly regarded as the Tourists' Gateway into Swaledale but there are other equally impressive routes into one of Yorkshire's wildest areas. The untamed places are seen best by approaching from Brough or Kirkby Stephen in Cumbria or via the Tan Hill Inn on the Durham border and then down to Reeth along Arkengathdale, but our favourite route to the Swale is from Hawes in Wensleydale through the famous Buttertubs Pass, and descending close to Thwaite between Keld and Muker. Natural phenomena and human activities have both left their mark on Swaledale. It was at Marske at the close of the Ice Age that the huge Stainmore Glacier from the Pennines ground its way into Swaledale along the channel of what is now Marske Beck and then melted to produce a long-evaporated but then substantial lake called Telfit. There was another huge lake at Ewelop between Grinton and Reeth, and perhaps the legend that the Romans first entered Swaledale by boat may just have some basis in fact.

But there can be no doubt about why the Romans came to Swaledale – they needed the lead. It is suggested that the Hurst mines were once used as a penal settlement and the lead obtained by the prisoners was exported to Rome and other parts of the Empire. The roof of St Peter's in Rome and also buildings in Jerusalem were sealed with Swaledale lead. It is also said that an iron ring, leaded into the rock, once secured restless prisoners.

After the Romans left round about 410 AD the Anglo-Saxons settled the area. In 672 AD the Venerable Bede wrote that merchants visited Catterick in order to bargain for lead with Swaledale miners. Then came the Scandinavians and the Danes who pushed their way inland from both the east and west coasts. Swaledale owes many of its place names and most of its dialect to the Scandinavians. By the time of the Normans an enormous quantity of lead was being exported from

Swaledale and was used to roof the Tower of London whilst some was exported to the Continent. During the 1980s we were fortunate enough to come across the diary of Edward R. Fawcett. Extracts have been used by students of mining in Swaledale, but not all of them have acknowledged his work. In 1985 we published his diary, which faithfully recorded the demise of an industry which in 1851 employed 1,129 miners, 41 smelters and 91 dressers and washers. In addition to this there would be those involved in the transport of the lead including carters, wheelwrights and blacksmiths, not to mention suppliers of food and ale. In the final quarter of the nineteenth century the industry collapsed mainly due to the import of cheap foreign lead. The redundant miners attempted to find new outlets for their skills. Some moved to the coalfields of Durham and Northumberland and others to the coalmines of Lancashire, which were favoured because their wives and families also found work in the booming cotton mills. Most never returned.

Edward R. Fawcett's father moved the family to Burnley in Lancashire to work in the coalmines and the 10-year-old Edward proved bright and eager, eventually studying at the Mechanics' Institute where he became the firm friend of Philip Snowden who later became Chancellor of the Exchequor. Edward was offered a place at London University but could not afford to go; he became a part-time teacher of Geology, Physiology, Astronomy and Hygiene.

Edward never lost his love of Swaledale and returned 'home' during the 1914-1918 war when a rise in lead prices allowed him to enter into a partnership to re-open the mines at Arngill and Ivelet. As the war ended the venture came to an end, but Edward set himself up as a draper and remained in the Dale, where he continued to compile his history of mining in Swaledale.

These days the income of the Dales comes largely from a combination of sheep farming and tourism, with many farms combining the two by offering bed and breakfast plus accommodation for touring caravans and tents. The Swaledale sheep is a tough beast and makes light of weather conditions which would decimate most other breeds. With its black and grey face, curled horns and tightly packed fleece the Swaledale

The Tan Hill Inn on the Pennine Way being given a facelift in 1990.

is unmistakeable and is the central feature of the annual agricultural shows at Reeth and Muker.

The steep winding road from Hawes into Swaledale passes the area known as Buttertubs, a small area of limestone on either side of the narrow pass for which there is limited parking. The name derives from the deep holes in the limestone which were said to be shaped like an old-fashioned buttertub. At their most impressive during heavy rain, the tubs are fringed by rowan trees and are fed by mini-waterfalls crashing down into the depths. Great care must be taken when viewing them.

It is not often realised that the Dales are an area of mountains, and nowhere is this more obvious than in Swaledale with Lovely Seat, 2,213 feet (675 m) and Great Shunner Fell, 2,340 feet (713 m), dominating the area. At the head of Swaledale stands Tan Hill Inn which, at an altitude of 1,732 feet (528 m), is the highest hostelry in England. We once visited on a hot August Bank Holiday only to find that a cheerful fire was crackling in the grate, and delighted visitors were commenting on how chilly it was on the raised rocky plateau above the Inn from which there are sweeping views down Swaledale and also into Durham. Carved into one of these flat rocks is a memorial to Susan Peacock who ran the Inn with an eccentric but respected hand from 1902 until 1937. Tan Hill Inn is still the site for the local shepherds' meet in May, and also lies directly on the Pennine Way, which encourages a steady stream of hungry and thirsty visitors. To cater for these the Tan Hill Inn was extended during 1990, but without destroying its character which was shown in the late Ted Moult's television commercial for double glazing.

Tan Hill is linked to Reeth via the six-mile-long, three-mile-wide Arkengarthdale, a side dale once given over almost entirely to lead mining but now becoming increasingly popular with naturalists. There is no mention of the dale in the Domesday Book, but it was part of Arkengarth Forest which linked with Stainmore Forest and which before the Conquest was owned by the Saxon Earls of Mercia. Once the Norman grip tightened on Saxon England, Arkengarthdale was given to Alan, the Earl of Richmond; around 1100 he placed Robert Arkhil in charge of the forest and it is his name which is perpetuated in several places. Arkhil Beck, for example, runs down the valley to join the Swale at Reeth and the village of Arkhill Town also carried his name. Arkhil Garth during the course of time became Arkengarthdale, so beloved of walkers who climb Water Crag, 2020 feet (615 m), Great Pinseat, 1914 feet (583 m), Hove, 1818 feet (554 m) and Windegg, 1600 feet (488 m).

In the valley are tiny villages with buildings constructed of worn-looking sandstone and bearing such fascinating names as Arkletown, Hurst and Booze. At Arkletown there was once a church constructed in 1145 but unfortunately demolished in 1818 and replaced by the church of St Mary at Langthwaite, although several interesting gravestones still remain. How Booze got its name is a mystery but lead miners were hard drinkers and Langthwaite men may have climbed the steep road to booze with the village locals. The Boozers and the Langthwaite-ites often had fierce fist fights and running battles along the street and up into the mountains. Others say that Booze originated as a prison camp for slave workers in the Roman lead mines. We would like to think that both were right! Visitors to Arkengarthdale should not fail to visit the C.B. Inn which takes its name from the Bathurst family who

A Swaledale Ram.

came to the Dale in 1656 when Dr John Bathhurst, who was Oliver Cromwell's physician, purchased extensive lands. His son Charles supervised the fortunes of the rich and famous C.B. mines and his name is also perpetuated in the C.B. Hotel. From this, one road runs up to the head of the Dale and another turns right to Barnard Castle in Durham. Whaw (pronounced Waar) is the last village up the Dale and in many ways it is the most typical. It stands on Arkle Beck and is overlooked by great scars on the hillsides marking the workings of Danby mine, one of the most prolific in Arkengarthdale. Fortunately, many of the old smelt mills now have preservation orders on them.

The Swale itself is said to be the fastest-flowing river in England and it can be lethal at times of flood. In June 1701 Grinton was badly damaged by flood water, and between 1642 and 1805 twenty people drowned in its swirling waters. On November 16th 1771 there occurred a very severe deluge which battered every bridge in Swaledale and actually destroyed most of them. Little has been done since that time to tame the wildness of the river, and on January 2nd 1976 considerable damage was done by flood waters. The name Swale is applied following the junction of Great Sleddale and Birkdale Becks. From its source the Swale flows seventy-two miles, almost half of this distance being a meander across the Plain of York, until it joins the Ouse between Lynton-on-Swale and Aldborough. In this chapter we shall follow the river as far as Richmond.

From its early reaches the peat-stained river sweeps rapidly down towards Keld which is the first substantial settlement in Swaledale. Its houses, like those of all the other villages of the area are built of warm yet often crumbling sandstone. A feature of the 1990s is the restoration work going on, but – alas! – too many buildings are destined to become holiday homes.

Keld, sited 1050 feet (320 m) above sea level, in a cul-de-sac just off the main road, is a tiny spot which always seems to have lots of visitors. The word 'keld' actually means a well or a spring, and this was obviously the reason for the settlement developing at this spot. Keld chapel served the spiritual needs of the upper dale before a church was established at Muker in 1580. Lovers of waterfalls should not miss Keld, for nearby are Catrake, Kisdon and Rainby Forces, only the first being on private land. Alongside the Pennine Way is Wain Walk Force, and like the others it can be thunderously impressive after rain. The area is dominated hereabouts by Kisdon which, despite its height of 1636 feet (498 m), means 'a little detached hill'. The Vikings who settled here valued the seclusion of the village but higher up is Keld Green, a much more recent settlement containing a former shooting lodge which is now a youth hostel.

The road downdale from Keld undulates to such an extent that Angram is the most elevated village in the Dale, being 1,185 feet (361 m) above sea level. Any ornithologists walking this area are in good company, for the village of Thwaite was the home and training ground for Richard and Cherry Kearton who were pioneers of wildlife photography, being involved in both still and movie techniques. The brothers were skilled in the production of hides enabling them to get close to

Buttertubs Pass.

the birds, and they even mounted a camera inside a stuffed cow! We were given many interesting facts about the Keartons by Miriam Wright, who is related to the brothers and also to Edward R. Fawcett. The Keartons dominate Thwaite, the view over the bridge bringing into focus a guest house and cafe named after them.

Richard was born in 1862 and took up a post with a London publishing firm in 1882, but was able to retire in 1898 and got an income from his own illustrated books on wildlife. Cherry was born in 1871 and was the more famous of the brothers, producing wildlife films both at home and abroad. He was well known for his radio broadcasts and was killed by a German bomb which fell outside Broadcasting House in 1940. Corner House Farm where they were born still stands. They must have watched the dippers beneath Scar House Foss, a lovely waterfall close to the village. Thwaite is not situated on the Swale itself but on a rapidly flowing tributary called Stock Beck. The main river runs alongside the road close to Muker.

The Keartons' early education was provided by the school at Muker which bears a plaque recording the life of each brother. 'Muker' derives from the Norse and means a cultivated enclosure. In the season this can be a hustle and bustle of a place full of gift shops, inns and tea shops, and on the second Wednesday in September parking can be a nightmare. This is the day of the annual show and sports, the main event being a lung-bursting fell race which attracts athletes from nearby and far afield. The village has a long history dating back more than 1500 years, but surprisingly there is no mention in the Domesday Book, presumably because there was no church until 1580. Its foundation ended the practice of transporting the dead along the still obvious Corpse Way down the dale to Grinton. It is at Muker that the road from Buttertubs descends into Swaledale, and it is just one more area to delight the walker. Footpaths lead upstream to Keld and downstream to Gunnerside, passing Ivelet Bridge. This is one of the finest packhorse bridges in the Dales and is said to be haunted by a headless dog.

Gunnerside is yet another old Norse settlement, its name deriving from Gunnars Seatre – the pasture of Gunnar. It is a short distance from the Swale and is set on another swiftly

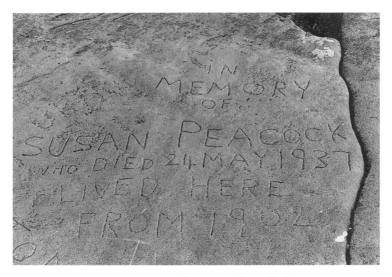

The memorial to the Tan Hill Landlady.

moving tributary – Gunnerside Gill – which arises on the slopes of the 2204 feet (671 m) Rogan's Sat. This was another of the lead-mining centres of Swaledale. The Old Gang Mines and the workings alongside Gunnerside Gill both attract large numbers of students of industrial archaeology, who follow the obvious footpaths up into the breezy uplands.

To reach Reeth, the next major settlement down the Swale, the road passes through three villages: Low Row, Feetham and Healaugh. It is difficult to tell when Low Row ends and Feetham begins but the early inhabitants must have been a religious lot, for set among a tangle of stout cottages surrounded by colourful summer flowers are two nonconformist chapels, the Melbecks church and a Friends' Meeting House. This was the home village, until his death in 1984, of the author Thomas Armstrong, famous for his novels *King Cotton* and *The Crowthers of Bankdam*. If you want to learn about local lead mining, you should read *Adam Brunskill*, which we feel represents Armstrong the storyteller at his best. Healaugh is Saxon in origin, and John of Gaunt once had a house here which he probably used as a hunting lodge.

Reeth is a large village standing at the junction of

Arkengarthdale and Swaledale, and here is the Swaledale Folk Museum, another establishment run by local volunteers. It is tucked away in a disused chapel but is clearly signposted from the central village green which is surrounded by a number of hotels including the Burgoyne, the King's Arms, the Buck, and the Black Bull. The Museum is open daily from 10.30am to 6pm between Easter and October 31st on payment of a small fee and at other times for parties of more than twenty by appointment only. On display is the history of lead mining, farming and other crafts practised over the centuries by the Dales folk.

Reeth crouches beneath the slopes of Mount Calver and was mentioned as Rie in the Domesday Book. Reeth Bridge, spanning Arkle Beck and built in 1773, is a good example of the work of John Carr, the famous York architect who constructed many bridges and houses, including Harewood House near the banks of the Aire between Otley and Leeds. Although a modern centre for tourists, Reeth has never been the religious focus of mid-Swaledale.

The parish church of St Andrew's at Grinton is less than two miles from Reeth and is often called the 'Cathedral of the Dales.' It is a building of impressive proportions, but it would have been full during the heyday of lead miners when the population of Swaledale was high. It was founded in Norman times and was once administered by the monks of Bridlington Priory. It has a chained Bible or rather a Birkett's New Testament on a fourteenth-century stand, a Jacobean pulpit and the Royal Coat of Arms of William and Mary dated 1693. Near to the south aisle there is a hagioscope, often referred to as a leper's squint. This enabled the afflicted to watch the Mass without infecting the congregation. On the porch there are grooves and scratches made when weapons were sharpened, and of particular interest is a memorial to Ann Barker who in 1692 was buried in linen rather than the wool which the law required in those days. For this offence her father Adam was fined the then substantial sum of £5, and this is the last such recorded prosecution. The law was designed to protect the staple and very lucrative wool industry on which the whole early English economy depended.

From Reeth onwards Swaledale assumes an altogether

The Old Gang Lead Smelt Mill, Swaledale.

different appearance, quite suddenly becoming greener and more fertile. Tucked in among the trees between Grinton and Richmond are the ruins of two nunneries, one the house of the black-robed Benedictines, the other belonging to the Cistercian order whose habits were woven from paler undyed raw wool. The two houses were sited about a mile apart but on opposite banks of the river, although the nuns could visit each other by crossing a substantial set of stepping stones. At one time there was a trow ferry across the river which consisted of a rowing boat pulled by a system of ropes attached to the bank. From Fremlington you can reach the village of Marrick; it stands on top of a hill with 375 steps leading down to the priory. For those who find the climb a problem it is possible to return to the village via a farm track. The priory is now used as a young people's Field Study Centre in contrast to Ellerton which, apart from its church tower, is now a ruin.

There is a local legend suggesting that tea was first drunk in England at Swale Hall on Harkerside Moor above Fremlington. James Raine and his wife are said to have boiled the tea with cream and sugar and the couple and their guests consumed the lot from earthenware bowls including all the leaves!

The remains of a small Roman camp have been discovered nearby; it was probably built on top of an older British settlement, but all the artefacts have been removed to museums at York and Darlington.

This area of Swaledale was dominated by religious houses between the twelfth and the early sixteenth centuries and within close reach of Richmond Castle there are three more establishments. St Martin's Priory dates from the early twelfth century and was an extension of the mighty Benedictine Abbey of St Mary's at York. It is on private land but the farmer who owns the site is most accommodating, although not much remains of the buildings which were suppressed in 1536. The west face of the tower with a decorated window and arches gives some impression of the abbey's former glory. In the centre of Richmond itself is a remarkable tower which is all that remains of the Franciscan Priory – the brethren being known as Greyfriars because of the colour of their habits. The perpendicular Gothic tower dates from the late thirteenth century.

After a walk of around a mile from Richmond along the banks of the Swale you come to the extensive ruins of the Premonstratensian Abbey of St Agatha at Easby which is open daily. The founder was Roald the Constable of Richmond, who gave land on which there may already have been the remains of a previous monastery. Historians cannot agree about the precise date of the foundation but the period between 1151 and 1155 would appear to satisfy most scholars. All abbeys belonging to this order are difficult to chronicle because for some reason they were exempt from episcopal jurisdiction and are therefore seldom mentioned in diocesan records which provide the main references. The Premonstratensian order was initiated in 1120 by St Norbert who founded an abbey or Pratum Monstratum at Laon in France. The first English abbey was set up at Newhouse in Lincolnshire in 1143, but Easby was the first Premonstratensian house in the North. During the thirteenth and fourteenth centuries these Northern abbeys were under threat from the Scots and must have thought that they had little to fear from English armies. The brethren of Easby, however, discovered quite the opposite. In 1346, on their way to fight at Nevillés Cross near Durham, English troops were billeted at the Abbey, and caused extensive damage. Easby was never a large abbey and when it was

The Folk Museum at Reeth.

dissolved in 1536 its net revenue was calculated at only £111 17s, 11½d. Although small, Easby has a rare beauty, and Pevsner described it as 'one of the most picturesque monastic ruins in the county richest in monastic ruins'. It also brings the added bonus of a parish church situated within its grounds. This pre-dates the abbey and is also dedicated to St Agatha, its serving priest having once been provided by the abbey. Inside the church is a replica of the Easby Cross, the original having been taken away to gather dust at the Victoria and Albert Museum. This fine example of Anglo-Saxon sculpture dates to around 800 and we feel it is a pity that it was not kept in its original place. The church, however, has other treasures which cannot be removed. These are mid-thirteenth century wall paintings which depict both Old and New Testament scenes.

Richmond, one of the finest market towns in Britain, owes its existence to the presence of a tough-looking Norman castle which actually saw little action over the centuries. The name Richmond derives from the Norman Riche-mont meaning a strong hill. Perhaps because it looked so strong perched on a rock over the Swale, invaders decided to leave well alone. Such a commanding site must have been in use before the Normans but hard evidence is not easy to come by. What is known as Scots Dyke along the eastern boundary of the town is probably an early British earthwork. A hoard of Roman coins was discovered on the castle bank in 1720. As there was a settlement four miles down the Swale at Catractonium, (Catterick) the coins may have come from there. Alan Rufus of Britany was influential in his second cousin William of Normandy's victory at Hastings and also helped to consolidate the invaders' hold over England. Alan's reward was a substantial gift of land which had once belonged to the Saxon Earl Edwin of Mercia, who had a house at Gilling West, three miles from Richmond.

In 1071 Alan built the first stone castle in England to tighten his grip over his new lands. The great Scollard's Hall, named after a favourite servant, has been floored and glazed and is of great architectural interest, and the 100-foot (30 m) high keep built a century later is also impressive. Scollard's Hall, built as early as 1080, may well be the oldest surviving domestic building in England. No doubt because it was never attacked, little effort was made to maintain the castle and in 1341 it was 'worth nothing in yearly return and sadly needing repair'. In 1538 things were even worse and apparently even the roof had fallen in. It also seems likely that the castle was never actually completed, but what it lacks in history it makes up for in folklore. It is said that beneath the castle King Arthur and his knights are sleeping, awaiting a call to arms to save the country. There is also said to be an underground passage leading to Easby Abbey in which lurks the ghost of a drummer boy who disappeared whilst exploring the tunnel. In 1910 the Ministry of Works, now Department of Environment, purchased the Castle from the Duke of Richmond, ensured its future and

The Church at Grinton-in Swaledale.

thus helped the town to develop into a major tourist resort. The castle is now administered by English Heritage and is open daily on payment of a fee. There are facilities for the disabled and regular events are held including musical entertainments, military displays and medieval combat.

Whilst the Castle is impressive, it appears to be somewhat truncated and lacks an outer bailey; in fact what has happened is that the town itself has been built over this area, and this accounts for the unusual layout. Most of the old town wall and its three gates – Frenchgate Bar, Fingle Street Bar and Briggate or Cornforth Bar – have vanished, leaving only their names, but in Friars Wynd there is just a fragment of the original defences.

Few towns have a more impressive market square than Richmond. Sloping and cobbled, it is dominated by the Chapel of Holy Trinity which looks like, but is not in fact, the parish church. Indeed it is not even a religious house these days and has functioned as an isolation hospital in times of plague, a school, a prison during the Jacobite uprisings, a courthouse and a brewer's warehouse – few buildings can have had such a varied history. In 1973 Holy Trinity became the museum of the Regiment of the Green Howards, underlining the fact that this is a military area with Catterick Camp on the outskirts of

Easby Abbey – one of Swaledale's finest monastic houses.

the town. The regimental museum is closed in December and January, but is otherwise open on weekdays, and between April and October it is also open during weekends. There is a small entry fee to view a display of the 300-year history of the regiment with a fine collection of medals, campaign relics, buttons and badges. The chapel itself, however, must be one of

Richmond Castle, Swaledale.

the strangest buildings to be found anywhere in the country. There is no churchyard, the tower is separated from the rest of the church by a set of offices, and there were once shops set into the aisles. No one seems to know why and how the chapel developed in this manner, or how a link with its Norman past has been maintained. In the tower there is a curfew bell which is still rung every evening and which once warned all residents to extinguish their fires to prevent the town burning down. Richmond also has a second museum, situated in Ryders Wynd, which concentrates on local history.

The parish church of St Mary was always outside the lower walls and sat on sloping ground above the river. It was extensively restored in 1860 by Gilbert Scott, but he sensibly retained the canopied choir stalls and misericords (carved seats). One of these depicts two pigs dancing to music played on the bagpipes by a third pig. The Green Howard regiment is also represented here by a magnificent memorial chapel. The comprehensive school opposite the church has an Elizabethan charter. Lewis Carroll (Charles Lutwidge Dodgson [1832-1898]) was a pupil here when it was a grammar school, and during that time his father was vicar of nearby Croft.

Richmond has an elegant Georgian feeling about it and our

161

favourite promenade is around the outside of the castle which provides exciting views down to the bridge, below which are delightful and safe cascades. The bridge was built by John Carr in 1789 to replace a structure destroyed by a flood of 1771. Its construction brought about a rather amusing controversy, as the Corporation would own the northern half of the bridge whilst the southern section was the responsibility of the County. Their wranglings delayed construction but we can understand the problems in dividing a three-arched bridge in two!

To complete the feeling of Georgian England, a visit to Richmond's theatre is essential, especially during an evening performance. The charming little theatre which seats only 237 people was built in 1788 but had closed by 1850 and was not restored until 1963. Fortunately the uses to which it was put during the intervening period did not destroy the fabric as it was floored at stage level and the pit was used as a vaulted wine cellar. These vaults were constructed within the original walls and were easily removed during the restoration, which was carried out with amazing skill. It was also used as a furniture warehouse, corn chandler's shop and as a salvage depot.

There is only one of the town's institutions more famous than the theatre and that is 'The lass of Richmond Hill' who herself often attended the theatre. She was apparently named Fanny I'Anson, the song being written by Leonard MacNally:

> I'd crowns resign
> To call her mine,
> The lass of Richmond Hill.

The lyric must have worked because the two were married and often visited the theatre together. Our lasting memory of the Theatre Royal, Richmond is how close the audience get to the action, and we could even smell the greasepaint, hear the performers breathing and see the sweat upon their brows.

In the parish church on the south wall of the chancel is a monument to Sir Timothy Hutton of the Marske family who died in 1629. It shows the knight, his wife Elizabeth and their children plus the coast of arms. From this we can tell that one of the sons married into the Yorke family whose mansion once dominated the area below the Castle and close to the river in

The Bridge over the Swale at Richmond.

the Burgate area. Some 35 acres (14 hectares) of this estate, now called Temple Lodge, is a private park dominated by the Culloden Tower. Built in 1769 by John Yorke, whose son fought in the battle, the octagonal tower shows the mock Gothick style of the period to perfection. 'Gothick' is a term used for the Georgian copy of the medieval architectural style.

The old railway station which closed in 1963 is now used as a garden centre. This ensures that it will survive as a monument to the Yorkshire architect G.T. Andrews. The line reached Richmond in 1848, as a branch of the York to Darlington route. No doubt the railway brought tourists to Richmond and it is yet another example of the failure to retain a steam link to a main line. At least part of the line has been saved and is now a footpath leading out towards Easby Abbey. Here we must leave the Swale to complete its journey to the Ouse, the Humber estuary and the sea.

All the Dales rivers save those in the Craven area and the Ribble eventually feed the mighty Humber, but each has its own characteristics which are sure to continue to attract appreciative visitors. We hope that this book enables them to enjoy the Dales even more. Here folklore, history and natural history all blend together in a surprisingly small area.

Further Reading

Bradley, Tom (1890) A Series of articles from the *Yorkshire Weekly Post* reprinted by the Old Hall Press in 1988: *The Wharfe, the Aire, the Swale, the Nidd.*

Brown, J.J. (1931) *Moorland Tramping in West Yorkshire* (Newnes)

Duerden, N. (1968) *Portrait of the Dales* (Robert Hale)

Duncan, J.E. and Robson R.W. (1977) *Pennine Flowers* (Dalesman)

Freethy, Ron (1986) *Northern Abbeys* (Countryside)

Freethy, Ron (1987) *British Ferns* (Crowood)

Freethy, Ron (1987) *The River Aire* (Countryside)

Freethy, Ron (1987) *The River Ribble* (Terence Dalton)

Gunn, P. (1984) *The Yorkshire Dales* (Century)

Hallas, C.S. (1984) *The Wensleydale Railway* (Dalesman)

Hartley, M. and Ingilby, J. (1956) *The Yorkshire National Park* (J.M. Dent)

Lee, B.H. (1987) *Exploring the Yorkshire Dales* (Countryside)

Lee, B.H. [Ed] *Lead Mining in Swaledale* – The Diary of E. Fawcett (Faust)
(Bradford Diocesan Board/Valbergh)

Morris, J.E. (1910) *The West Riding of Yorkshire* (Methuen)

Raistrick, A. (1976) *Buildings in the Yorkshire Dales* (Dalesman)

Raistrick, A. (1968) *The Pennine Dales* (Eyre Methuen)

Raistrick, A. (1972) *Prehistoric Yorkshire* (Dalesman)

Riley, W. (1921) *A Village in Craven* (Herbert Jenkins)

Slack, M. (1984) *Portrait of West Yorkshire* (Robert Hale)

Thackrah (1977) *Ilkley* (Dalesman)

Ward Lock's Red Guide (1968) *The Yorkshire Dales* (Ward Lock)

Yorkshire Naturalists' Union (1971) *The Naturalist's Yorkshire* (Dalesman)

Index

Addingham 84
Airedale 58
Aire river 3, 89
Aire springs 49
Airton 53, 54-56
Aldborough 110
Alum Pot 43, 44
Angram 137, 150
Appersett 89
Appletreewick 80
Arkengarthdale 148-149
Arkhill 148
Arkletown 148
Arncliffe 73
Askrigg 1, 92-93
Austwick 13, 19, 26, 29, 41
Aysgarth 94-96

Bainbridge 67, 90-92
Barden Bridge 82
Barden Tower 82
Beamsley 84
Beckermonds 67
Beverley 4
Birkdale Beck 150
Bishopdale 69
Bolton abbey/priory 9, 16, 52, 62, 80,
  82-83
Bolton Castle 93-94
Bolton Woods 16
Booze 148
Boroughbridge 110
Bridlington Priory 154
Brimham rocks 121, 130-131
Buckden 69
Buckden Pike 69
Burnley 146
Burnsall 75, 79-80
Buttertubs Pass 151, 152
Byland Abbey 138

Calton 52, 55-56
Cam Beck 71
Cam Fell 67
Caperby 93

Catrake Force 150
Catterick 145
Chapel-le-dale 19, 30
Clapham 1, 19, 20-26
Colt Park 14, 43
Conistone 75
Cotterdale 89
Cotter Force 89
Coverdale 71, 98, 140
Coverham Abbey 9, 100-101
Cray 69
Crummockdale 41

Darlington 77, 156
Dead mens hill 140
Deepdale 68
Doe river 26, 29, 30

Easby Abbey 156-157, 160
East Witton 98-99
Ellerton Priory 155
Embsay abbey/priory 82
Embsay steam railway 62-65, 77
Ewelop 145

Feetham 153
Feizor 19
Fleetmoss 68
Fossdale 89
Fossdale Gill 3
Fountains Abbey 48, 51, 80, 114-118
Fountains Fell 52
Fountains Hall 56
Foxup 68, 73
Friars Head 56
Fremlington 155
Furness Abbey 43, 44

Gaping gill 21, 25
Gargrave 19, 52, 56-58
Gayle 90
Giggleswick 2, 31, 35-36, 40, 52
Giggleswick school 22
Glasshouses 136
Goredale Scar 2, 50-51

Grassington 7, 9, 13, 14, 63, 73-78, 83
Grass Woods 14, 74
Great Shunner Fell 2, 147
Great Whernside 71, 72, 121
Greenfields 68
Greenhow 136
Greta river 2, 26, 29
Grinton 145, 154-155, 159
Gunnerside 152

Hardraw 3, 89
Harrogate 118-119, 121
Hawes 45, 68, 69, 89, 90-91
Healaugh 153
Hearn Beck 3
Hellifield 19
Helwith Bridge 40, 41
Hornby 29
Horse Head Pass 68
Horton-in-Ribblesdale 2, 11, 41,
   42-43, 68
Hove 148
How Stean Gorge 140-141
Hubberholme 67, 68-69
Humber river 45
Hurst mines 145, 148

Ilkley 62, 71, 84-86
Ingleborough 19
Ingleborough cave 21, 25
Ingleton 1, 2, 19, 25, 26-28, 45, 67
Ivelet Bridge 152

Jervaulx Abbey 9, 42, 98, 100-101

Keighley 19, 57
Keld 150
Kendal 57
Kettlepot Ganister 10
Kettlewell 71, 73, 77
Kidstones Pass 69
Kilnsey 71, 72-73
Kingsdale 30
Kirkby Lonsdale 19
Kirkby Malham 51-54
Kirkby Stephen 145
Kisdon 150
Kisdon Falls 150
Knaresborough 118, 119, 121-130,
   131
Knuckle Bone 69

Lancaster 30
Lands Fell 89
Langcliffe 36-40
Langstrothdale 67, 68
Langthwaite 148
Lawkland 19
Leeds to Liverpool canal 52, 57
Leyburn 97-98
Lightwater Valley 110
Ling gill 44
Linton 75, 76, 78-79
Little Whernside 121
Littondale 15, 68
Long Preston 19
Lovely Seat 147
Low row 153
Lune river 29

Malham 13, 51-52
Malham Cove 2, 48-50, 52
Malhamdale 3, 89
Malham tarn 47-49
Marmion lower 107
Marrick Priory 155
Marske Beck 145
Marston Moor 130
Masham 105-107
Middleham 35, 101-105
Middlesmoor 141
Mossdale 89
Mouth-of-Hell see Alum Pot
Muker 147, 150, 152-153

Nappa Hall 93
Newby 19
Newby Cote 19
Newhouses 44
Nidderdale 1, 2, 110, 121-143
Nidd Head 121
Nun Monkton 121

Old Gang Lead Mines 155
Otley 86
Oughtershaw Beck 68
Ouse river 67, 110, 150

Parcevall Hall 80
Pateley Bridge 2, 121, 131-134,
   136-137
Penyghent 19, 41, 42
Pikedaw 52

Ramby Force 150
Ramsgill 138
Rayside 25
Redmire 94
Reeth 145, 147, 153-154, 157
Ribblehead 34, 44, 45
Ribble river 3
Richmond 30, 155, 156-163
Richmond castle 9, 158-159, 161
Ripley 121, 130
Ripon 107, 110-114

Salley Abbey see Sawley Abbey
Salt Lake City 44
Sawley Abbey 40
Scaleber 36
Scar House 137-139
Sedbergh 27
Selside 2, 43
Semerwater 92
Settle 2, 19, 31-34, 45
Skell river 110
Skipton 2, 19, 57-64, 83
Skirfare river 72-73
Smelthouses 136
Snape 109
Stainforth 40-41
Stainmore glacier 145
Starbottom 69-70
Strid the 82, 83
Stump Cross Caverns 1, 7, 132-136
Summerbridge 136
Swaledale 7, 9, 110, 145-163
Swale river 3, 149

Tan Hill 9, 10, 147-148, 153
Tarn dub 44
Telfit 145
Thornborough Circle 110
Thorpe-in-the-Hollow 80
Threshfield 9, 77
Thwaite 150-152
Trowgill 25
Twiss river 26, 29, 30

Ure river 3, 45, 89ff

Victoria Cave 3, 36-37

Wain Wake Force 150
Waldendale 71
Water Crag 148
Wenning river 29
Wensley 96-97
Wensleydale 89-110
West Burton 94
West Tanfield 107
Wharfedale 1, 3, 58, 110
Wharfe river 45, 67
Wharfe village 41
Whernside 19, 45, 121
Widdale 89
Widdale Beck 89
Wild Boar Fell 2
Windegg 148
Windermere 71

Yockenthwaite 67
York 77, 121, 141, 156